UK Timeline
for Family History

Angela Smith
Neil Bertram

The Book Forge
TBF

UK Timeline for Family Historians

ISBN 978-0-9571287-0-5

© 2012 Text and pictures Angela Smith and Neil Bertram.

First published 2012.

Published by:
The Book Forge
www.thebookforge.org.uk
admin@thebookforge.org.uk

British Library Cataloguing in Publication Data. A catalogue record for this book is available from the British Library.

Every effort has been made to substantiate the facts and records in this book. However, neither the authors nor the publishers can be considered liable for any omissions or errors.

Printed in the United Kingdom.

Dedicated to our families who we have bored to death with family history!

Our grateful thanks to Debbie, Judith, Allan and other friends and family who have kindly read through earlier drafts of this book and offered their comments.

Introduction

Once upon a time, many years ago...... well that's just the whole point; 'many years ago' – just who can remember all those dates? Don't answer that – some of us have to have them written down......

So, this handbook has been compiled as a tool for the family historian and in particular those new to genealogy or whose knowledge (or memory) of dates is shaky. It is not meant to be an exhaustive list of historical events. Rather, this timeline offers a guide for family historians to refer to and to help set dates into a wider historical context. It is selective; we have included items that we think are particularly important for family historians to know but there are many more that have not been cited. We have, for example, numerous references to the various taxes that have been imposed down the centuries since the paper trail for their collection might name your ancestor. There are many additional taxes that could be included – a tax on wallpaper for example in 1712 and another on the use of bricks in 1784, for which some records survive.

The main column on each page lists events pertinent to family historians where there *may be* some traceable record. Items in italics may not yield any records but are of interest to family historians. Some items only have the briefest of descriptions but the reader should be able to easily find more detailed information on events or source records by using the phrases in an internet search engine. Inclusion (*or not*) does not necessarily imply that some sort of traceable record is available.

Two smaller columns may be found on the edge of each page. These include a column listing English monarchs and prime ministers: 'Monarchy, State and Church'. The reader will find further information of a more general nature in the adjacent column which will hopefully offer some historical context: 'Socio-cultural'.

We have indicated, in a few places, if original records are kept in The National Archives (TNA), in local record offices (LROs) or in specialist niche repositories like The Imperial War Museum. We have avoided giving too many specific details as these can be easily found by the reader using keywords in an internet search engine.

All population numbers are approximate - averaged from several sources as nobody seems to agree! Talking of numbers: yes, you are correct; there are no page numbers throughout this book. This is entirely intentional; just too many numbers otherwise.

The future looks bright for Family Historians! More and more records are being made available all the time; especially at the moment as records for workers across many diverse trades are being released for general viewing. Keep searching and if they are not there today they just maybe tomorrow.

We really do hope you find the information useful in some way. Even if you find one nugget of information that prompts you to search new areas for your ancestors or offers some context in which to place their situation. Happy searching!

Throughout this book we have used pictures from our family albums and places we have visited on our travels. If you think you recognise someone please feel free to contact us - we may be related!

Angela and *Neil*

Angela has a PhD in Combined Historical Studies (Warburg Institute, London) and is a freelance lecturer. 35 years ago she could be found walking to school with Neil. Now both have been reunited through their love of digging up the past.

Neil has worked in publishing most of his life except a ten year period driving a London Taxi.

Abbreviations

BL	British Library
DNB	Dictionary of National Biography
EU	European Union
FFHS	Federation of Family History Societies
GRO	General Registry Office
LSE	London School of Economics
HMC	Historical Manuscripts Commission
LRO	Local Record Office/Archive
NAI	National Archives of Ireland
NAS	National Archives of Scotland
NRA	National Register of Archives
ONS	Office for National Statistics
OPCS	Office of Population Censuses and Surveys
OPS	Office of Public Sector Information
PRO	Public Record Office, formerly in Chancery Lane, now part of TNA
SPCK	Society for the Promotion of Christian Knowledge
TNA	The National Archives
VCH	Victoria County History

1000s

1066
After his conquest of England, William the Conqueror began re-distributing land, granting tracts across England to his Norman followers and also the church.

Norman barons often adopted the name of their lands in England (and Normandy) as surnames.

1086
The *Doomsday Survey* was collated. It was the earliest systematic survey of land ownership in England and gives details of land owners and the status of individual tax payers. It is available online and in print.

1100s

1100s
The guild system begins to develop.

Large numbers of farmers from the Low Countries came to settle in the area of The Wash.

1127
The first documented evidence for heraldry occurs when Geoffrey Plantagenet is knighted. Thereafter the art of heraldry begins to develop.

1130
A series of financial records kept by the Exchequer for the Crown known as Pipe Rolls are introduced. They record Exchequer payments and names of tenants.

Surnames begin to be used more widely by landowners to assert their rights to hereditary property.

Socio-cultural	Monarchy, State and Church
1066 Battle of Hastings	**1066** (to 1154) House of Normandy
Extensive programme of castle building	**1066** (to 1087) **William (I) the Conqueror**
	1070s (to c1220) Growth of monasticism
	1077 First Cluniac priory at Lewes
1096 (to 1099) First Crusade	**1087** (to 1100) **William (II) Rufus**
1100 Population 2 million	**1100** (to 1135) **Henry I**
1119 Knights Templars founded	**1106** Augustinian (black) canons establish their first abbey near Colchester
	1124 (to 1153) King David I (re-unites Scotland)
	1128 First Cistercian abbey founded at Waverley
	c1130 The Gilbertines founded
1135 Outbursts of anti Semitic violence	**1135** (to 1154) **Stephen**

Left timeline column

1139
(to 1149)
Civil war as Matilda fought Stephen for the crown

1143
The first Premonstratensian house in England

1154
(to 1399)
House of Plantagenet

1154
(to 1189)
Henry II

1170
Murder of Thomas Becket, canonised in 1173

1171
High Kingship in Ireland ended (when Normans invaded)

1189
(to 1199)
Richard I (The Lionheart)

1199
(to 1216)
John

Second timeline column

1144
(to 1149)
Second Crusade

1149
Oxford University founded

1170
Population of London exceeds 30,000

1189
(to 1192)
Third Crusade

1189
and **1190**
Massacres of Jews in London and York

Right text column

1139 (to 1149)
Period called The Anarchy.

1155
The weavers were granted a royal charter making them the oldest livery company in London.

1161/2
Danegeld tax finally abolished.

1167
The beginnings of Oxford University. Names and place of birth of alumni have been published.

1170s
Anglo-Norman nobles permitted to take lands in Ireland.

1187
The judgments pertaining to land ownership called Feet of Fines begin, and are a source for surnames.

1188
The travels of Gerald of Wales, whose notes have been published, and offer detailed observations on the Welsh landscape and life.

Saladin Tithe levied in England to provide funds for the Third Crusade.

1189
Legal records survive from the late 12th century. Some have been published. These include the Curia Regis rolls which record the business of the court held before the king's justiciars and the Assize Rolls which record dealings of courts at local level.

1199 (to 1517)
Charter Rolls begin recording royal grants issued by the Chancery.

1200s

Early 1200s
Manorial records recording administrative details of estates begin. Their use is widespread by the end of the century.

1202
The Patent Rolls start which contain a record of royal correspondence (letters patent). They are a useful source for tracing individuals in the Middle Ages.

1204
Close Rolls begin which record grants made by the monarch to individuals and groups.

1200s
The first monumental brasses are used in English churches to commemorate the dead.

1209
Beginnings of Cambridge University. Names of alumni have been published.

1226 (to 1426)
Liberate Rolls begin recording payments made by the Crown to various individuals associated with the (very large) royal household such as stipends and pensions. The rolls offer particularly detailed information for the mid 13th century.

c1240 (to 1660)
The earliest Inquisitions Post Mortem (escheats) date from this period. They are useful for tracing inheritance of property, family descents and alliances especially between 1270 and 1350.

c1250
First map of the British Isles drawn by Matthew Paris. (BL)

1200
Population 3.5 million

1202
(to 1204) Fourth Crusade

1204
Jersey separates from Normandy

1204
King John imposes English laws concerning property and inheritance on the Irish

1213
(to 1221) Fifth Crusade

1215
Magna Carta

1216
(to 1272) **Henry III**

1221
Dominicans (black friars) arrive in England

1224
Franciscans (grey friars) arrive in England

1228
(to 1229) Sixth Crusade

1230s-1240s
Oxford and Cambridge Universities granted Royal Charters

1242
Gunpowder introduced into Europe

1248
(to 1254) Seventh Crusade

Timeline (left column)

1259
Normandy surrendered to France

1264
Battle of Lewes brought Simon de Montfort to power as the 'uncrowned King of England'

1264
(to 1267) Civil War

1265
Simon de Montfort's Parliament called in opposition to Henry III

Simon de Montfort killed at the Battle of Evesham

1267
(to 1272) Eighth Crusade

1271
Marco Polo reaches China

1271
(to 1272) Ninth Crusade

1272
(to 1307) Edward I

1277
(to 1296) New towns, Flint and Harlech, planted adjacent to Edward's castles in North Wales

1278
All Jews in England imprisoned, almost 300 were executed in London

1283
Wales comes under English control

Main column

1254
An assessment of the clergy was undertaken for taxation purposes. Returns for eight dioceses survive: Bangor, Durham, Ely, Lincoln, Llandaff, London, Norwich and St Asaph.

1266
The earliest freemen rolls date to the mid 13th century with the first admission to the City of Exeter dating to 1266. The Exeter Rolls are almost continuous from 1286 to the present.

1272
The Husting Rolls (court records for the City of London) survive almost complete from this date.

Some of the earliest court rolls, including those for the Duchy of Lancaster, date from c1272; also Fine Rolls, which record payments to the Crown for grants and privileges.

Later 1200s
Parliamentary statute brings change to the feudal system of land ownership.

1279
A series of land surveys called the Hundred Rolls were made (named after the hundreds by which most returns were recorded). This was a form of census that recorded the adult population of England and Wales and services due to manorial lords. A few survive in TNA, including those for Kent, and have been published.

1285
Statute of Winchester. Local guards were organized to question strangers and to patrol towns and town walls at night in an effort to maintain peace. In addition every man was

required to serve the king in the event of a rebellion or a foreign invasion.

1288 (to 1292)
The Pope permitted King Edward one-tenth of the ecclesiastical income of England and Wales to pay for a crusade. A survey (digitized and available online) was made called the *Taxatio Ecclesiastica* which lists 8,500 churches and chapels across the country.

1290
Records of the Mayor's Court for the City of London survive from 1290.

1290 (to 1334)
Lay Subsidy Rolls begin recording the taxes imposed on the laity (commoners). The rolls are a very important source for the local historian with names recorded.

1300s

1315 (to 1317)
The Great Famine in England (and across northern Europe) from 1315 until 1317 and again in 1321 after bad weather caused poor harvests. Consequent widespread unrest and criminal activity (including infanticide).

1300s
Many Flemish weavers were encouraged to settle in England during Edward III's reign.

Social mobility increases in England as the rigid class structure of former times is gradually challenged not least through the growth of a mercantile middle class.

1341
A valuation for taxation purposes was carried out called the *Nonarum Inquisitiones*. The

1287
Massive storms altered parts of the coastline (Old Winchelsea was destroyed)

1288
Piepowder Courts set up to try offenders at local fairs and markets

1290
Statute of Quia Emptores

1290
King Edward's Edict of Expulsion effectively expelled all Jews from England, around 16,000 left the country

1295
First legally elected legislature; the Model Parliament

1296 (to 1357)
War of Scottish Independence

1300
Population 5 million

1306 (to 1329)
Robert the Bruce of Scotland

1307 (to 1327)
Edward II

1314
The Scots, led by Robert the Bruce, rout the English at Bannockburn

1326
First Scottish Parliament

1327 (to 1377)
Edward III

1337 (to 1453)
Hundred Years War against France begins

1337
The rank of Duke created

Timeline (left column)

1347
Calais captured and settled

1346
Battle of Crecy

1349
Ordinance of Labourers inaugurates English labour law

1350
Population 3 million

1351
The Statute of Labourers put into effect the earlier Ordinance of Labourers, preventing workers from moving in search of work and instituting stocks

1360
Treaty of Brétigny

1369
Famine in England

1370s
Emergence of peasant farmers (yeomen class) with up to 100 acres

1377
(to 1399)
Richard II

Main text (right column)

results, which cover many counties, have been published.

1349 (to 1350)
Massive reduction in population numbers as a result of bubonic plague – as many as one third of men, women and children perished.

1350s
Widespread movement of labourers and their families following the Black Death (bubonic plague) as workers sought (and could charge) more for their labour.

1350
Status of Children Born Abroad Act permitted children born abroad to two English parents to be English.

1354
Churchwarden accounts for Ripon in Yorkshire are amongst the earliest to survive.

c1360
The oldest surviving road map of Great Britain called the Gough Map is produced – now in the Bodleian Library in Oxford.

1377
Langland writes his poem *Piers Plowman* that offers much information about medieval farming practices.

1377, 1379 and 1381
A Poll Tax levied on almost every individual in the land except paupers. In 1377 those eligible were aged 14 years and above, in 1379, 16 and above and in 1381, 15. Two-thirds of the poll tax returns survive (TNA). They frequently give names and the relationships between taxpayers. Some lists included the names of heads of households as well as servants.

1377 (until 1875)
Earliest records for the Court of Common Pleas (or Common Bench) survive covering all actions between individuals that did not involve the king.

1382
Winchester College is founded; records of alumni survive and have been published.

1384 (to 1858)
Earliest wills proved by the Prerogative Court of Canterbury.

1388 (until 1972)
Quarter Sessions begin, dealing with legal issues at local level, which meet four times a year. Records usually in county record offices though few survive before the later 1500s.

The Statute of Cambridge restricted the movement of labourers and beggars and made county hundreds responsible for their own poor.

A survey of guilds and local fraternities was produced. The returns are held in TNA; those written in English have been published.

1400s

1400s
By early 1400s, most people in England would have used surnames that passed to their children. Hereditary surnames developed later in Wales.

1429
The right to vote was given to all men over 21 years or owning freehold land.

1441
First documented black African slaves brought into Europe.

1381
Peasants Revolt, prompted by Poll Tax, occurred in towns and countryside

1384
John Wycliffe, religious reformer and Bible translator, dies

1386
The Wonderful Parliament

1387
Chaucer starts *The Canterbury Tales*

1399
(to 1461)
House of Lancaster

1399
(to 1413)
Henry IV

1400
Population 3 million

1400
(to 1415)
Welsh revolt led by Owen Glendower

1413
(to 1422)
Henry V

1415
Battle of Agincourt

1422
(to 1461)
Henry VI

1434
River Thames freezes

1437
Assassination of King James I of Scotland

1440
Rank of viscount created

Timeline (left column)

1453
Loss of all French lands except Calais

1461
(to 1470)
House of York

1461
(to 1470)
Edward IV

1470
(to 1471)
House of Lancaster restored

1470
(to 1471)
Henry VI

1471
(to 1485)
House of York restored

1471
(to 1483)
Edward IV

1483
(April to June)
Edward V

1483
(to 1485)
Richard III

1485
(to 1603)
House of Tudor

1485
(to 1509)
Henry VII

1509
(to 1547)
Henry VIII

Timeline (second column)

1455
Gutenberg invents the printing press

1465
Irish living near English settlements made to take English surnames

1471
Battles of Barnet and Tewkesbury

1485
Battle of Bosworth

August-October: severe outbreak of sweating sickness in London kills thousands

1492
Christopher Columbus reaches America

1498
Vasco da Gama reaches India

1513
Battle of Flodden Field

1517
Sweating sickness kills thousands particularly in Oxford and Cambridge

Rise of Lutheranism

Main column

c1450
A map of Goole Moor (Inclesmoor) and Thorne Moor in south Yorkshire was made in connection with a land dispute. (BL)

1450
Jack Cade's Rebellion - against the policies of Henry VI; including the Statute of Labourers.

1483/4
The College of Arms was founded to regulate heraldry and the granting of armorial bearings.

1489
An Anti-Enclosure Act was introduced to discourage land enclosure that was causing de-population in some rural communities and was a major contributory factor in the desertion of villages.

1494
Vagabonds and Beggars Act permitted punishment of the poor.

1495
Licensing of alehouses begins.

1500s

1509
Government documents known as the State Papers, Foreign and Domestic have been published for the reign of Henry VIII and subsequent monarchs down to the late 18th century. They cover numerous social as well as political issues and name thousands of individuals. They have been published in calendar form.

1514 (to 1854)
Trinity House issues pensions to seamen and their families. Registers are extant from 1727.

1516
A second Anti-Enclosure Act.

1522
Muster Rolls begin, listing adult males who were available for military service.

1523
The Great Subsidy was levied on all individuals over 16 years of age with land or goods worth £2 or an annual income of £1 or more. The returns contain very full lists of taxpayers. The original records are in TNA; some have been published.

1525
Admiralty records survive from 1525.

1530
The Egyptian Law was passed to prevent gypsies from entering England and Wales and introduced discrimination to those already here. Further act passed in 1554.

1530 (to 1688)
Heraldic visitations began to be undertaken across the country. Many have been published and provide a wealth of information for genealogists.

1530s (to c1700)
Inventories of personal estate often compiled for probate purposes. Many survive.

1535
A thorough survey of church wealth, *Valor Ecclesiasticus* ('church valuation'), was made by royal officials in preparation for the Dissolution of the Monasteries. Applied to churches in England and Wales, plus parts of Ireland under English control.

1535 (and 1542)
The Welsh legal system incorporated into the English system and English administrative practices introduced by the Laws in Wales Acts.

1519
Ferdinand Magellan began his circumnavigation of the world

1525
Rebellions in the eastern counties due to Amicable Grant

1528
Sweating sickness kills thousands across England and spreads to Europe

1534
Reformation of the English church begins

1535
Beard tax imposed

1535
Laws in Wales Acts begin

1536

The Pilgrimage of Grace rebellion, prompted by opposition to the Dissolution, began in Lincolnshire and the East Riding; 200 rebels were later executed

1538

The Exeter Conspiracy – an attempt to depose Henry VIII and replace him with a Yorkist; Henry Courtenay, 1st Marquess of Exeter

1540

Thomas Cromwell executed

1536

Divorce made possible in Scotland through the Commissary Court of Edinburgh.

A poor law act passed allowing vagrants to be whipped.

1536 (to 1539)

The Dissolution of the Monasteries began whereby the small religious houses and later the larger ones, were systematically closed. Many monks and nuns found themselves homeless and the closure of religious houses exacerbated poverty as work opportunities and alms-giving dramatically decreased. Some 650 religious houses across England and Wales were closed.

Many redundant buildings (former monasteries, nunneries and so on) sold and others given away by the king. Many minor noble families benefited. As much as one third of former church land across England and Wales was absorbed into royal and private hands.

1538

Thomas Cromwell charges all clergy in England and Wales to keep records of all baptisms, marriages and funerals at which they officiated. *Boyd's Index* lists some 3.5 million English marriages from 1538-1837.

1539

John Leland begins his journeys through England and Wales published as *The Itinerary* in five volumes.

1540

Statute of Wills permits freehold land in England and Wales to be bequeathed and sets a legal age for the writing of a will at 14 years for males and 12 for females (spinsters and widows only). Repealed and superseded by the Wills Act of 1837.

1542
The Crowns of Ireland Act, passed by the Irish Parliament, declaring that the new Kingdom of Ireland belonged to the monarchs of England. Parliaments of Ireland and England remain separate.

1542 (to 1830)
Court of Great Sessions established in Wales to meet twice a year to administer English law.

1547
The Statute of Legal Settlement provided for the branding or enslavement of beggars who were deemed capable of work. Beggars incapable of working were to receive relief.

Many grammar schools founded during the reign of Edward VI for the teaching of boys.

1549 (to 1550)
A tax on sheep was levied though repealed within a year. Some records of ownership survive, though a proposed national census of sheep was never completed. The records can prove very useful when parish registers are unavailable.

Book of Common Prayer introduced a new liturgy in church.

1551 (to 1552)
Gypsies required a licence in order to travel.

1552
The Alehouse Act led to the recording of licensees' names.

In Scotland all parishes were ordered to keep registers of baptisms and marriage banns. This was extended to include burials from 1565 and actual marriages from 1616. Adherence was patchy and few registers survive before the late 1600s.

1543
Copernicus published his *On the Revolution of Heavenly Spheres*

1547
(to 1549)
The Western Rebellion concerned protests in the southwest against the enforcement of Protestantism

1547
(to 1553)
Edward VI

1549
Kett's Rebellion was a protest in Norfolk against enclosure that culminated in more than 3000 deaths

1551
Last known serious outbreak of sweating sickness

1551
Scotland: General Provincial Council orders each parish to keep a register of baptisms and banns of marriage

1552
Foundation of Christ's Hospital, Horsham, the first bluecoat school

1553
(to 1554)
Wyatt's Rebellion; a protest against the marriage of Queen Mary to Philip of Spain

1553
(9 days)
Lady Jane Grey

1553
(to 1558)
Mary I

1553
Catholic practices
in church were
re-introduced

1554
(to 1558)
Philip
in the right of
his wife Mary

1555
Establishment of
Muscovy
Company for
trade with Russia

1558
(to 1603)
Elizabeth I

1558
England loses
possession
of Calais

Protestant
practices in
church restored

1561
Elizabeth I issues
the first patent

1554
Deportation of gypsies to Norway. Death penalty imposed on gypsies who remain in England for more than a month.

1555
Toll Books introduced at horse fairs recording buyers' names and where they came from.

1558
Recognised as the start date for parish records despite the fact that the instruction to keep registers had been given twenty years earlier. Parish records were now kept on parchment so the survival rate is greater than those previously recorded on paper.

1558 (to 1563)
Statute of Artificers were a series of laws that were introduced to regulate labour issues. They included the setting of wages and placed limits of the free movement of workers. The statute was abolished in 1814.

1559
The Act of Uniformity laid the basis for the Protestant Church in England. Parishioners were required to attend church on Sundays.

Thousands of Flemish (Walloon) and Dutch immigrants settled in London and the eastern counties during Elizabeth's reign, especially after the Dutch revolt of 1567, bringing with them their cloth-making skills.

Another Poor Law Act differentiated types of poor.

1560
In Scotland, Roman Catholicism is disestablished as the state church and replaced by the Church of Scotland which would later be based on Presbyterianism.

1560 (continued)
In Scotland, probate jurisdiction was transferred from church courts to secular Commissary Courts under the Principle Commissariat of Edinburgh.

1571
The holdings of each parish now regularly recorded. Surveys of land belonging to the church and inventories of ecclesiastical property known as glebe terriers were widely produced.

1572
Many Huguenots come to England in the wake of the Massacre of St Bartholomew's Day in France.

1573
Humphrey Llwyd's map of Wales *Cambriae Typus* published.

1574
A Scottish poor law act instituted some of the provisions made in English poor law.

1576
Justices of the Peace can issue bastard orders (Bastardy Bonds) whereby the father of an illegitimate child would be required to pay maintenance for its support.

Lambarde's *Perambulation of Kent* published. This is the first county history with much of genealogical interest.

In Guernsey, a register of contracts was established including land transactions. Records are in French.

Another Poor Law act authorised counties to establish 'houses of correction' for vagrants and beggars, and set out the 'Punishment of the Mother and reputed Father of a Bastard'.

1563
Major epidemic of bubonic plague in London

1569
Northern Rebellion

Mercator created his map

1570
Population 4.1 million

1570s
(to 1580s) Development of Presbyterianism

1572
Thomas Howard, 4th Duke of Norfolk, tried for treason for his part in the Ridolfi plot to restore Catholicism in England

1577
Sir Francis Drake sets sail from England to circumnavigate the world

Late 1500s
The art of cartography develops as instrumentation improves.

1579
Christopher Saxton completes a series of detailed and elaborate county maps for England and Wales. Saxton's maps were used by subsequent mapmakers.

1581
Recusancy (non-attendance at Anglican services, especially by Catholics) becomes a criminal offence punishable by heavy fines. Names of recusants appear in Quarter Sessions records and from 1587-1606 in Assize Court records. Defaulters were listed in the Recusants' Exannual Roll of 1581-1634/5.

1580
Congregationalists emerge as a Puritan sect called Brownists

1582
The Gregorian Calendar begins to replace the Julian Calendar across Europe, adjusting dates by 10 days, shortening the year slightly and revising the pattern of leap years. Many countries had already standardized 1 January as New Year's Day. Reforms were not applied in England, Wales and Scotland until 1752. Adopted in parts of Ireland but under English influence, its use there died out by the 1640s.

1582
Establishment of Edinburgh University

1585
Anglo-Spanish war begins

1586
The first large-scale settlement of English people to Ireland occurred called the Munster Plantation.

Camden's *Britannica* published – the first topographical survey of England.

1586
Famine in England

1588
English speaking colony established on North American island of Newfoundland.

1588
Spanish Armada

1590

Chetham Chest Fund was established to pay pensions to Navy personnel. Records survive from the early 1650s.

1592 (to 1691)

Annual Recusant Rolls of convicted Catholics compiled by the Exchequer. They are particularly extensive from 1663 to 1670 with over 10,000 entries, although these include many Protestant dissenters too.

1597

The Relief of the Poor Act required Churchwardens and overseers in each parish to levy a tax on parishioners in order to fund the provision of work for the poor; to assist those who couldn't work and to find apprenticeships for the young.

Male vagrants could now be drafted into naval service.

1598

Copies of all parish records were now to be sent annually to the local bishop. The copies are called Bishops Transcripts and are useful when original parish registers have been lost or damaged.

1600s

1600

Scotland adopted 1 January as New Year's Day instead of 25 March as in England and Wales and most of Ireland. It continued to use the Julian Calendar.

1601 (to 1834)

The Poor Law placed a legal responsibility on each parish to care for those unable to work. Many records survive recording information on payments to the poor

1590
(to 1591)
North Berwick witch trials

1595
Nine-Years War begins in Ireland against England

Battle of Cornwall - Spanish raid during the Anglo-Spanish War

1597
Dublin gunpowder disaster

Witchcraft hysteria in Scotland

1597
Future King James I writes his views on witchcraft; *Daemonologie*

1600
East India Company began to trade in the Far East

Population 4.8 million

1601
Robert, Earl of Essex executed for treason

including rate books recording local rates paid by parishioners, Settlement Certificates, Bastardy Bonds, nonconformists etc. The act also introduced parish apprenticeships for poor and orphaned children.

1602

Richard Carew's *Survey of Cornwall*. Available for free online.

The Land Registry is established in Jersey; with records in French.

1604

A revised set of church laws, Book of Canons, decreed that parental support was required for those less than 21 years to marry. In addition, the canons codified the system of granting licenses to marry necessitating an applicant to provide a bond and an allegation (or affidavit). Such bonds and allegations were filed and those that survive provide details about age, marital status and so on that is invaluable to the family historian. The records after 1660 are particularly complete. They are usually to be found in local archives.

1606

This year saw the beginnings of the Ulster Plantation as thousands of Protestants began to colonise north-east Ireland. At first this occurred privately but by 1609 the project had royal support and it is estimated that nearly 20,000 people settled. Concurrently many existing settlers moved within Ireland looking for land that better suited them.

1600s

Some records available from the early 17th century for the first indentured servants who went to the New World for work.

1602
(to 1795)
Dutch East India Company founded

1603
(to 1649)
House of Stuart

1603
Epidemic of bubonic plague in London

1603
(to 1625)
James I

1603
Union of the Crowns of Scotland and England though the nations remain separate with their own Parliaments

King James created many new peerages to encourage loyalty

1604
One third of the population of York die from plague

1605
Gunpowder plot

1606
Great tidal surge in the Severn

Guy Fawkes executed

Adoption of Union Flag for Great Britain

1607
The Midland revolt

Jamestown established in Virginia, America; one of 13 colonies founded by the English before 1733

1609
Bermuda settled by the English.

1611
John Speed publishes *The Theatre of the Empire of Great Britaine* which included the first set of individual county maps of England and Wales plus maps of Ireland and a general map of Scotland. Speed's maps include hundreds, inset maps and some town plans.

1615
Penal transportation of miscreants to colonies in North America and the West Indies is more regularly used. Alphabetical lists of convicts who were transported between 1614 and 1775 have been published.

1617 (to 1858)
Register of Sasines recorded land conveyance in Scotland, in effect the first public register of deeds.

1618
A hundred destitute children were transported from London to augment the colonial population of Virginia.

1620
One hundred Puritan separatists later dubbed the 'Pilgrim Fathers' sail for America on the *Mayflower* establishing Plymouth Colony.

1622
The island of St Kitts sees the first English settlement in the Caribbean. Barbados became an English colony in 1627, Nevis in 1628 with more in the following decades. Between 1640 and 1660 over two-thirds of English emigrants to the Americas would live in the West Indies, most in Barbados and many being indentured servants.

1611
King James Bible published

1612
Trial of the Pendle Witches

First Baptist congregation established in London

1615
Arbella Stuart, England's 'lost queen', starves herself to death in The Tower of London

1616
Death of William Shakespeare

1617
Death of John Napier; Scottish mathematician who invented logarithms

1618
Sir Walter Raleigh executed

1621
James I gives Canada to Sir Alexander Sterling

1622
First record of bottled spring water at Holy Well Spring, Malvern

Timeline (left column)

1625
(to 1649)
Charles I

1626
Acidic waters at Scarborough lead to an interest in the benefits of 'taking the waters' and development of other spa towns

1630
Population 5.6 million

1630s
Public stagecoaches began to provide links with London within a 30-mile radius of the city

1634
The Irish House of Commons passes an Act for the Punishment of the Vice of Buggery

Main column

1622 (to 1641)
The first English newspaper called the Weekly News begins. Foreign news only.

1628 (to 1862)
Records of Fleet Prison, Marshalsea Prison, King's Bench Prison and Queen's Prison begin. (TNA)

1630
Muster Rolls for Ulster, arranged by county.

700 Puritans left Southampton for America settling in Massachusetts. Some 20,000 more will emigrate to New England in the 1630s, the peak of the 'Great Migration'. By 1700 the population had reached 92,000.

1634
In Ireland, all Protestant baptism, marriage and deaths were to be recorded in Church of Ireland registers. Where parishes complied, often marriages were also included. Many Catholic and other Protestant churches unofficially performed these rites for their members, but few such records survive from before the early 19th century.

The Stent records of Inverkeithing dating from 1634 are amongst the earliest Scottish land valuation documents to survive.

The colony of Maryland was established in America, to provide a refuge for Catholics, although many settlers would be Protestant.

1634 (to 1640)
Charles I's Ship Money Tax was levied without parliamentary support and with mixed results. It was a tax on property designed to raise funds for maritime defence and was traditionally levied on coastal towns. From the mid 1630s this very unpopular tax was levied countrywide. Many tax schedules have

survived (in BL and LRO) and name individuals. A few schedules have been published.

1641 (to 1642)

As a result of the many plots against King Charles and unrest in Parliament, a Protestation Oath was introduced. The act required all adult males in England and Wales to declare allegiance to the king, Parliament and the Protestant religion. The names of those who refused to sign were noted. About one third of returns survive (in the House of Lords) and have been published. Counties are listed alphabetically and then by parish and hundred; some counties are better represented than others.

1642

The Collection for Distressed Protestants in Ireland lists many women and records oaths of loyalty made to the king. The returns, of which about one third survive (also in the House of Lords), were organized by parish.

Civil war interrupts keeping of parish registers.

1642 (to 1660)

The Committee for Advance of Money and Compounding tax was established to investigate the wealth of individuals for the purposes of forcing loans. After August 1646 only Royalists were forced to pay.

1643 (to 1664)

The Committee for Plundered Ministers was established to investigate the political loyalties of church ministers and increasingly acted against those men who supported King Charles. The Sequestration Committee was also set up to confiscate the property of Royalists who continued to fight for the king.

1641
Irish Rebellion

Newspapers which included news from home begin to proliferate as censorship ends

---

1642
Unrest in Ulster; 50,000 killed

1642
Oxford is the royal base until 1646

1642
(to 1626)
English Civil War begins

1643
Birth of Isaac Newton

1643
Licensing Order passed by Parliament to censor newspapers

1643 (to 1664) (continued)
The Committee for Compounding with Delinquents dealt with issues concerning the recovery of sequestrated property belonging to Royalists who agreed not to take up arms against Parliament. (TNA)

1644
First register of the Congregational Church.

1646
The abolition of The Court of Wards and Liveries brought wardship and other ancient feudal practices to an end.

1647
London Corporation established to build workhouses and houses of correction for the indolent poor, to enforce laws against vagabonds and to set the poor to work.

1648
Quakerism begins, founded by George Fox; registers of members were regularly kept by the 1670s.

1650
Repeal of the Act of Uniformity led to the rise of many non-conformist groups.

1651
The Battle of Worcester brought an end to Civil War. Some 8,000 Scottish soldiers captured at Worcester were deported to the Americas to work as indentured labourers.

Approximately 3.7% of the English population and 6% of the Scottish died as a result of the Civil War.

1652
Cromwell's opponents were stripped of land in Ireland under the Act of Settlement. The lands were re-distributed.

1645
Battle of Naseby left the Royalist army shattered

1646
Westminster Confession of Faith

1647
Earliest Baptist registers survive from this date

1648
(to 1649) Second Civil War

1649
Execution of Charles I

As the Commonwealth Period begins, many Royalists flee abroad

1650
First coffee house in London

1651
Charles II crowned at Scone but goes into exile

1650s
Ireland loses a quarter of its population - from 1.3 to 1 million owing to the effects of the Cromwellian wars

1652
First Anglo-Dutch War, mostly fought at sea

1653

During the Commonwealth, civil registers of births, marriages and deaths officially replace parish registers of baptisms, marriages and burials in England and Wales although some parish registers continued to be kept. Few civil registers survive from this period.

Provincial probate courts abolished with probate now granted in London only.

1653 (to 1660)
Civil marriage introduced by the Marriage Act.

1654

A register survives (in print and online) of names of 10,000 indentured servants who left from the port of Bristol for the New World between 1654 and 1686. Servants came from all over Britain.

1655/6

The Down (or Civil) Survey was carried out which mapped Ireland. The original maps were lost to fire but copies survive in various collections and have been published.

1656

The Edict of Expulsion rescinded, officially permitting a small community of Sephardic Jews to live in London; owing to Cromwell's need of their financial assistance.

1657

Earliest surviving Roman Catholic registers but few were kept before 1700 and most date from after the late 18th century. In Ireland, Catholic registers were not widely kept until the 1830s.

1659

Pender's Census in Ireland recorded the names of owners and details of land

---

1653
(to 1660)
The Protectorate

1653
(to 1658)
Oliver Cromwell makes himself Lord Protector of the Commonwealth of England, Scotland and Ireland

Barebones Parliament

1654
(to 1660)
Anglo-Spanish War caused by commercial rivalry

Jamaica captured from the Spanish

1656
Musaeum Tradescantianum, the first museum open to the public established in London

1658
Hurricane storms in southern England; the worst for centuries

1658
(to 1659)
Richard Cromwell now Lord Protector

holdings. Surviving records have been published.

Start of monthly national meteorological Mean Central England Temperature data collection; available online.

1660

A poll tax was levied on all men and women over 16 years of age annually until 1697.

Commonwealth registers end, parish registers resume and provincial probate courts were re-established.

Records for Naval Officers begin after administrative re-organisation by Samuel Pepys.

A few British begin to settle in the Dutch-controlled Cape Colony in South Africa.

The first regular standing army established.

1660 (to 1902)
Naval passing certificates, awarded to officers on their successful completion of examinations, were inaugurated.

1661

A (voluntary) tax entitled A Free and Voluntary Present to Charles II was levied for which returns for more than 30 counties survive.

1661 (to 1828)
The Corporation Act prevented non-Anglicans from holding municipal office by requiring oaths of allegiance to the Crown and Church of England and the annual taking of Anglican communion.

1662

The Quaker Act required individuals to swear an oath of allegiance to the king.

1660
(to 1707)
House of Stuart restored

1660
(to 1685)
Charles II

1660
Many new peerages were created by King Charles II including dignities granted to his mistresses and their families

1661
Bodies of Oliver Cromwell and Henry Ireton exhumed and posthumously executed

---

1660
The Royal Society founded to promote the discussion of matters of scientific interest

First entry in Samuel Pepys' diary

1661
The Post Office introduces post marks

1662 (continued)

An Act of Uniformity passed this year led to the establishment of many places of education for nonconformists including Bristol Baptist College.

The Settlement Laws came into force permitting newcomers to an area to be evicted if a complaint was made against them within 40 days of arrival. The law reduced the mobility of the poorer classes and discouraged those without work to search for employment elsewhere. If a man left his own parish, he had to take a Settlement Certificate with him which guaranteed that his home parish would cover any return costs that he might incur if he began to claim poor relief.

The Settlement Act also required gypsies to be baptised.

Limits to rights to claim poor relief.

1662 (to 1689)

A Hearth Tax imposed by Parliament to support King Charles and his household. A shilling was to be paid twice yearly for every hearth (or stove) in all domestic dwellings. Subsequent amendments, permitted exemptions. From 1663 all hearths whether taxable or not, were listed. The tax returns reveal the size of dwelling in which the payee lived.

1664

The Conventicle Act forbad religious meetings of more than five people in an effort to discourage non-conformity.

1664 (to 1815)

Impressment to the navy was now officially authorised.

1662
Bury St Edmund's witch trials

1662
Charles II sold Dunkirk to France

Clarendon Code (included the Act of Uniformity) required all English and Welsh clergy to accept the Book of Common Prayer

1664
(to 1667)
Second Anglo-Dutch War – England captured New Netherland and renamed it New York

1665

Oxford Gazette (later called *The London Gazette* and still in circulation) founded; carrying much of interest to the genealogist including a record of appointments to public office and issues of insolvency.

A non-conformist burial ground called Bunhill Fields opened in London.

Later 1600s

Gravestones are now regularly used to mark place of burial in churchyards.

1666 (to 1814)

The Burial in Wool Act meant that woolen shrouds were now to be used, with a £5 fine for non-compliance, though paupers were exempt. Parish registers were often annotated to show payment or exemption. The directive tended to be ignored from the 1770s.

1667 (to 1853)

The earliest Ships' Muster Books begin recording financial issues and act as a form of service record. (TNA)

1668 (to 1920)

Naval Officers' Pay Books. (TNA)

1669

First Lutheran registers kept.

1670

Divorce by act of parliament is introduced in England and Wales, but just 318 successful cases were heard by 1858; only four cases were brought by women. Annulments and separation decrees were available through church courts, but decrees did not permit re-marriage.

Earliest Synagogue registers.

1665
Five-Mile Act - restrictions on nonconformist ministers

1665
Great plague of London kills more than 60,000 – the last serious visitation of plague in England

1666
Royal Court returns to London after the Great Plague

1666
Great Fire of London

1667
Dutch raid on River Medway

John Milton; *Paradise Lost*

1669
Samuel Pepys records the last event in his diary

1670
British Hudson Bay Co founded leading to the establishment of trading posts in Canada

Population 5.7 million

1672

Charles II's Royal Declaration of Indulgence in March loosened some of the strict laws against nonconformists. Certain penal laws were suspended and the building of some non-conformist chapels was permitted.

In Scotland, workhouses were to be established for the employment of able-bodied beggars. Charity workhouses were later founded for the relief of those individuals who could not work.

1673

The Test Act came into force, enhancing the regulations imposed by the Corporation Act of 1661 and ensuring that non-conformists could not hold public office. The Act was frequently renewed leading to various 'Returns of Papists' over the next hundred years.

An act was passed permitting the calling of special constables on a temporary basis in response to a rise in public disorder.

1673 (to 1849)

Naval succession books introduced to ships – listing warrant and commissioned officers. (TNA)

1674

Records for the Old Bailey begin and are useful for the detail they provide of defendants, their lawyers and witnesses Proceedings up to 1913 are available online.

1675

John Ogilby's *Britannia Illustrata* includes 100 strip maps of the chief roads in England and Wales.

1672
(to 1674)
Third Anglo-Dutch War – British Army increased to 10,000 men

1672
High Court of Justiciary established in Scotland

1674
Treaty of Westminster ends the Third Anglo-Dutch War

1675
To curb political activity King Charles issues the 'Proclamation for the suppression of Coffee Houses'

1676

1676
Charles II and Louis XIV sign secret treaty

The Compton Census, named after Henry Compton, Bishop of London, attempted to find the numbers of Anglican conformists, Roman Catholic recusants and Protestant dissenters in England and Wales. Information was collated by ecclesiastical parish. The returns have been published and some (including those for Norwich) are available online.

1676 (to 1772)

The Ordinary of Newgate's Accounts begin. They are detailed records made by the chaplain (or Ordinary) of Newgate prison and relate, for example, final conversations with criminals. They are available online.

1677

Samuel Lee's list of merchants living in and around London published.

1679

The Royal Hospital Kilmainham in Dublin was founded to house retiring soldiers and to administer the pensions of those leaving service in Ireland.

1682

The first English settlers arrive in the province of Pennsylvania after its establishment the previous year by Quaker, William Penn.

Travels of Celia Fiennes (to 1712) whose diaries have been published and provide detailed information on English towns and properties she visited.

1685

The Edict of Nantes was revoked by the French king, Louis XIV which resulted in the renewed persecution and killing of many Huguenots; thousands fled to England to

1678
(to 1681)
The conspiracy to assassinate Charles II, fabricated by Titus Oates, led to the execution of 15 men and widespread anti-Catholic hysteria

1680
The Great Comet was the first to be discovered by a telescope

1684
Severe weather conditions: a Frost Fair held on the River Thames

1685
(to 1688)
James II

1685
Monmouth Rebellion

Bloody Assizes

escape persecution. Registers of Huguenots begin.

1687
The Settlement Act of 1662 was amended as it now became necessary to establish settlement by occupying a property valued at more than £10 per annum, for more than forty days.

1689
The Toleration Act permitted nonconformists to worship; provided they licensed their meeting places.

1691 (to 1856)
Naval ratings pay books begin. (TNA)

1692
The Royal Hospital, Chelsea, London, was founded to house retiring soldiers and to administer the pensions of those leaving military service in Britain.

1693 (to 1963)
A new Land Tax was introduced after a county valuation was carried out, to assess who and what was taxable. A few early returns survive, though most postdate 1780. (TNA and/or LRO)

1694
Army introduces regimental numbers instead of being named after the colonel in charge.

The Bank of England was founded by Royal Charter.

1695
Parliamentary Act enacts fines on those who fail to inform the parish minister of the birth of a child.

First Dissenter lists in parish registers

1686
Isaac Newton writes *Mathematical Principles of Natural Philosophy*

1688
Glorious Revolution

1688
William III (to 1702) and **Mary II** (to 1694)

1689
(to 1692) Jacobite uprising in Scotland in support of the exiled James II and VII

1690
Battle of the Boyne

1692
Massacre at Glencoe

1694
(to 1699) Poll Tax imposed in Scotland

1694
William now rules alone after the death of Mary from smallpox

1695
Martin Martin; *A Description of the Western Islands of Scotland*

1695
Parliament does not renew the statutes requiring press censorship

recording the names of children born but not christened in the Anglican church.

The Royal Naval Hospital at Greenwich, London was founded.

1695/6
Marriage Duty Act levied a tax on births, marriages and deaths and charged a poll tax on unmarried bachelors! Surviving records name householders and dependents.

1696
The Great Re-coinage

Turnpike trusts proliferate as road travel increases

1696
Following a plot to assassinate King William, Association Oaths were introduced requiring all those in public office (civil, religious and military and all adults in some British colonies) to swear loyalty to the Crown. Many others, including some women, appear voluntarily on the Oath Rolls. Some records are available online.

County Sheriffs were now required to compile poll books recording the names of those who had voted in elections. The lists also indicate which candidate the voter supported. The elector's address and property entitling his vote is sometimes recorded. The survival rate for poll books improves after 1711.

Bristol Corporation of the Poor formed by local Act for the purpose of the setting up of workhouses. Other places later followed this example; Exeter in 1697 and Colchester in 1698.

1696
Genealogist Gregory King calculated that 63% of the population lived in poverty

1696 (to 1851)
A Window Tax replaced the Hearth Tax leading to widespread bricking up of windows. Occupiers of dwellings were eligible to pay the tax rather than owners. A few records for England and Wales survive though many survive for Scotland.

1697
An act authorises the erection of inscribed waymarkers on roads

697
*Marriage Act directed that all interfaith
…arriages would be considered as Catholic.*

… further Settlement Act extended and
…eveloped the system of granting certificates
…nd made it possible for the migrants to
…sist removal whilst looking for work.

698 (to 1703)
*… tax imposed on entries in parish registers.
…escinded after five years.*

700s

702
…rmy lists begin – for officers. (TNA)

*…irst daily newspaper – The Courant
…ublished on a daily basis until 1735 when it
…as merged with The Daily Gazetteer.*

704
…he Penal Code barred Catholics from
…oting, education and the military.

… Deeds Registry was established in the
…/est Riding of Yorkshire. It contains over
… million records of property ownership.
…he registry was followed by the East Riding
… 1707, Ireland in 1708, Middlesex in 1709
…nd the North Riding of Yorkshire in 1735.

708
…arliest artillery muster rolls. (TNA)

709
… March the Act for the Naturalisation of
…oreign Protestants was passed, by which
…nmigrants could pay a small fee in order to
…ecome naturalised. It was directed
…pecifically at French Huguenots who had
…ome to Britain and whom the government
…as keen to support.

1698
SPCK established
to foster better
manners and
encourage
establishment of
charity schools

1701
Population
6 million

1702
(to 1707)
Anne

1702
Many new
peerages created
by Queen Anne

1703
The Great Storm
causes severe
damage across
southern England
and kills 10,000

1705
Newcomen
patents a
steam engine

1707
Act of Union
establishes the
Kingdom of
Great Britain

1708
Abortive
invasion by the
Old Pretender

1708
(to 1709)
The coldest
winter in centuries

1709
Poor harvests
and famine
across Europe;
bread riots
in Britain

1709
The Tatler
founded

Early 1700s
The Gin Craze
causes extensive
social problems

1712
Last trial
for witchcraft
in England

1713
Treaty of Utrecht

1714
(to 1901)
House of Hanover

1714
(to 1727)
George I

1714
Jethro Tull
perfects the
seed drill

1715
(to 1716)
First Jacobite
rebellion mostly
in Scotland

1709 (continued)

Between May and November, some 13,000 'Poor Palatine' immigrants from German speaking lands arrived in England. Many were unskilled agricultural labourers and their arrival caused disquiet. Some were transported to North America.

1710

The first policy registers made in connection with fire insurance in London begin. They give the names of policyholders, details of the properties insured and any tenants. Registers can be found in local record offices and the Guildhall in London has a good collection.

1710 (to 1804)

A Stamp Act introduced a tax on apprentice Indentures, except where the fee was less than 12d and with a few other exceptions. The indentures often name the father of the apprentice together with his address and occupation.

1711

John Ecton published his *Liber Valorem et Decimarum*, a directory of ecclesiastical benefices which lists patrons and incumbents.

1714

The Hanoverian accession leads many Germans to settle in England and an increase in Anglo-German relations.

1715

Register of Papist Estates, established to facilitate additional taxation or forfeiture. Most entries survive up to 1725. The register was in force until 1778 and not fully abolished until 1791. Also from 1716, wills of Catholics were registered in the Close Rolls.

1715 (continued)

In Ireland, county militias were established with membership restricted to Protestants.

1718

Penal Transportation Act introduces the official removal of convicts to lands overseas. Between 1718 and 1776, more than 50,000 convicts were transported to North America. Transportation to America ended when war began between Britain and American colonists.

The Edinburgh Courant newspaper, with national coverage, was now published regularly. Followed by *The Caledonian Mercury* in 1720.

1723

Knatchbull's Act, The Workhouse Test Act, enabled workhouses to be erected by parishes.

Universal oath of loyalty imposed.

1724 (to 1726)

Daniel Defoe's compilation of observations *A Tour through the whole island of Great Britain* published.

1731 (to 1868)

The Gentleman's Magazine published: an invaluable source for contemporary society, including details of individuals.

1732

Earliest cavalry and infantry muster rolls. (TNA)

Unmarried mothers now expected to name the father of their illegitimate child under oath.

1717
The Masonic Grand Lodge of London and Westminster established

1719
An abortive Jacobite invasion, supported by the Spanish

1720
Widespread speculative investment in previous years collapsed with the South Sea Bubble ruining many families

1721
(to 1742)
Sir Robert Walpole, Whig

1723
The Black Act added 50 capital offences to the penal code, including some forms of poaching

1727
(to 1760)
George II

1728
Vitus Jonassen Bering reaches Alaska

1730
Severe famine in Ireland

1730s
Development of first seaside towns including Brighton and Margate

Timeline (left column)

1733
The Sugar and Molasses Act is passed to tax British colonists in North America

1733
Kay's flying shuttle invented

1735
(to 1749)
The Hawkhurst smugglers active

1738
Dick Turpin hanged

1739/40
The Great Frost across Britain

1740
(to 1741)
Severe famine in Ireland led to thousands of deaths and fuelled food riots

1742
(to 1743)
Earl of Wilmington, Spencer Compton, Whig

1743
(to 1754)
Henry Pelham, Whig

Main column

1733
Public records are now written in English rather than in Latin as had been the case.

1734
Brown and Kent's *Directory of the Cities of London and Westminster and the Borough of Southwark* published.

1739
Formation of Methodist Societies in and around London; though official break with Anglicanism came in 1784.

The *Scot's Magazine*, originally called the *Edinburgh Magazine*, was founded which includes birth, marriage and death notices and is still published.

1740
Protestant Householder returns made in Ireland. Transcripts of the original records survive for the counties of Antrim, Armagh, Down, Donegal, Londonderry and Tyrone and lists the names of heads of households and are arranged by barony and parish.

1741
The Foundling Hospital opened in London, with outposts elsewhere, housing some 27,000 children until 1954.

Earliest Moravian register for Fetter Lane congregation in London.

Scottish church registers begin.

1742 (to 1837)
The Baptists, Presbyterians and Independents form a General Register of births of Protestant Dissenters of the Three Denominations. In 1768 baptisms were added.

1744

An illegitimate child, who previously took the parish of birth as its place of settlement, now took the same place of settlement as its mother. This prevented mothers and children being separated if they became paupers.

1747 (to 1782)

A tax was imposed on all horse-drawn carriages, legislation which was extended in the early 1770s to cover steam-powered vehicles.

1751

Army regiments given official titles such as the 'King's Own'.

1752

14 September – England and Wales adopt the Gregorian calendar, thus moving from Wednesday 2 September to Thursday 14 September. The start of the year moves from 25 March to 1 January (New Style). Beware when interrupting dates!

Forced removal of tenants in the Scottish Highlands begins. Some 20,000 emigrate over the next decade and many move into the burgeoning cities such as Glasgow.

1753

Jew Naturalisation Act permitted Jewish people to become naturalised as British citizens but was repealed after one year due to widespread opposition.

The Licensing Act inaugurated the recording of full registers of victuallers - to be kept by the Clerk of the Peace at Quarter Sessions.

1754

Hardwicke's Marriage Act was introduced to counter irregular or clandestine marriages. Now, a marriage was *supposed* to take place

---

1745
Jacobite Rebellion in Scotland

1746
Battle of Culloden

1747
Liverpool and Bristol grow due to slaving activities

1750
Two earthquakes in London in the spring, cause panic

Population 6.5 million

1752
Parliament passes a bill to bestow estates forfeited by Jacobites to the Crown

1753
Foundation of the British Museum

Bow Street Runners appointed to patrol London's streets

1754
(to 1756) Duke of Newcastle, Thomas Pelham-Holles, Whig

in the parish in which either the bride or groom had been born. Each party was to be 21 years of age or to have parental consent. All couples (except Jews and Quakers) had to marry in a licensed (Anglican) church. Ready printed books for: name of bride and groom, their parishes, current marital status, date of ceremony, names of witnesses and officiating minister. Banns or marriage license recorded either with marriage record or separately. Irregular Marriages continued until 1949 in Scotland at, for example, Gretna Green.

1754 (to 1879)
First printed Annual Army Lists produced.

1756 (to 1777)
A tax introduced on silver plate for which some returns survive. (LRO)

1757 (to 1831)
The Militia Act revived county militias. Extensive military records survive from this date. Annual lists were made in each parish of all adult males between the ages of 18 and 50. Names, occupation, infirmities and, after 1802; number of children listed. By this act 30,000 men were raised between 1757 and 1763.

1761
Parliamentary Land Enclosure Acts (c1750 to c1845) increase as landowners seek to legalise enclosure of their property. The character of the landscape and its accessibility by the ordinary person were transformed.

1761 (to 1994)
Army records children born to serving soldiers.

1762
A parliamentary act required that records were kept within metropolitan parishes of parish poor infants.

1755
Lisbon earthquake causes tsunami in Cornwall three metres high

1756
(to 1757)
Duke of Devonshire, William Cavendish, Whig

1756
Seven Years War begins against France

Britons die in the Black Hole of Calcutta

1757
(to 1762)
Duke of Newcastle, Thomas Pelham-Holles, Whig

1758
England begins to govern in India, laying the foundations of the Empire

1760
(to 1820)
George III

1760
The Industrial revolution underway

1761
(to 1830)
The Bridgewater Canal is the first to open followed by a period of 'canal mania'

John Harrison's chronometer was perfected, allowing determination of longitude at sea

1762
(to 1763)
Earl of Bute, John Stuart, Tory

1762 (continued)
First Unitarian registers.

1763
Mortimer's Universal Directory (for London) included lists of shops.

Sketchley's Directory of Birmingham published.

1764
Army regimental records begin. (TNA)

1765
Benjamin Donn produced a detailed map of Devon (one inch to the mile), with maps of other west country counties in following years.

1766
Religious census of Ireland. Church of Ireland clergy were ordered by the Irish House of Lords to compile complete returns of all heads of households in their parishes.

Hanway's Act required that all pauper children under 6 from metropolitan parishes be sent to school in the countryside. This meant children were separated from parents.

1770
Records of prisoners kept from 1770 to 1894. (PRO)

1772
The British Nationality Act allowed citizenship to be assumed if the father was British.

First Navy Lists published.

First *Morning Post* published on a daily basis until 1937.

Elizabeth Raffald's *Directory of Manchester and Salford* published, listing traders, manufacturers and some inhabitants with appendices listing officials, carriers etc.

1764
Hargreaves invents the Spinning Jenny

Lloyd's Register of Shipping

House numbering introduced to London

1769
Captain James Cook claimed New Zealand for Britain

Arkwright invents the water frame used in textile production

1770
Captain James Cook reaches Australia

1771
First water powered mill heralds the beginning of mass-production in factories

1770s
A rise in grain prices saw the potato begin to usurp bread as a staple of the working-man's diet

---

1763
(to 1765)
George Grenville, Whig

1765
(to 1766)
Marquess of Rockingham, Charles Watson-Wentworth, Whig

1766
(to 1767)
Earl of Chatham, William Pitt the Elder, Whig

1767
(to 1770)
Duke of Grafton, Augustus Fitzroy, Whig

1770
(to 1782)
Lord North, Frederick North, Tory

1773
Captain James
Cook reaches
Antarctica

1775
Watt's steam
engine patented

American War of
Independence

1778
Louis XVI of
France declares
war on
Great Britain

1780
The Gordon Riots
erupt in London
in protest against
the Catholic
Relief Act,
hundreds died

1773
Edinburgh's earliest directory published.

1774
Madhouse Act – in force until Mental Health Act of 1959, required that all madhouses were to be licensed. The act was designed to counter abuses including the imprisonment of those who were not insane but had been rejected by their spouse.

1776
Arthur Young's *Tour in Ireland* published. Early copies included much social detail.

1777 (to 1852)
A tax imposed on male servants. Schedules are to be found in TNA and NAS.

1778
Catholic Relief Act. Lifting of anti-Catholic laws in England, Wales and Ireland. In Scotland, The Protestant Association prevented similar legislation. (See also 1791)

1779
The Penitentiary Act authorizes state prisons in preference to transportation or the death penalty.

1780
Pallot's Marriage Index records 1.5 million marriages celebrated in many parishes until 1837 covering most London parishes and some further afield. (Available online)

Pallot's Baptism Index records some 200,000 baptisms in Greater London up to c1837. (Available online)

Methodist registers begin.

c1780 (to c1842)
Bankruptcy case files available at TNA.

1782
Gilbert's Act allowed parishes to form unions to maintain workhouses to house the elderly and infirm.

First issue of Steele's Navy List gives names of serving officers. Superseded by Navy Lists in 1814.

1783 (to 1794)
Stamp Duty Act introduced a tax on baptisms, marriage and burials. It did not apply to paupers, and parish registers were often annotated to show payment or exemption. The introduction of the tax resulted in a fall in the number of entries overall, but an increase in the number of those described as paupers.

The Treaty of Paris creates the United States. About 75,000 people loyal to Britain leave America, mostly settling in Canada.

Glasgow's earliest directory published.

1784 (to 1807)
A Game Tax was levied on all qualified to kill or to sell game.

Taxes imposed on the owners of horses used for transport and racehorses. Both repealed in 1874.

The Window Tax levied in England and Wales was now introduced to Scotland where to this day blocked up windows are called 'Pitt's Pictures' after the prime minister who oversaw its introduction.

1785
First edition of *The Times*.

1785 (to 1792)
A tax on female servants for which some schedules survive in TNA and NAS.

1783
Volcano Laki in Iceland erupts with catastrophic consequences for European weather and leading to many deaths in late summer

1784
The threshing machine invented

Many Sunday schools open catering for poor children

First mail coaches

1782
(to 1782)
Marquess of Rockingham, Charles Watson-Wentworth, Whig

1782
(to 1783)
Earl of Shelburne, William Fitzmaurice, Whig

1783
(to 1784)
Duke of Portland, William Bentinck, Whig

1784
(to 1801)
William Pitt The Younger, Tory

Timeline (left column)

1788
The Dolben Act regulates slave trade

1789
The French Revolution begins – French émigrés arrive

1790
John McAdam invents a new surfacing treatment for roads

1792
First Regency Crisis

1792
Ross-shire riots in July (Year of the Sheep) when tenants protested against Highland Clearances

1793
(to 1802) Britain at war against France

1794
Treason trials

Main column

1788
First convicts and free settlers arrive in Australia.

Hasted's *History of Kent* (to 1799).

1791
Catholic Relief Act. Further relaxation of anti-Catholic laws which applied to England, Wales and Scotland. Similar legislation took effect in Ireland in 1793. (See also 1778)

The *Universal British Directory* published in five large volumes. The directory was a forerunner to the VCH and included geographical and historical details on counties as well as notes on schools and other facilities plus lists of inhabitants with trades. Subsequent copies list street directories and names of householders.

1792
A wave of emigration to North America from Scotland occurred as thousands were forcibly evicted from the land.

1793
In response to the French wars, the Aliens Act was introduced (another in 1798) which established a system of registering aliens at ports of entry. Registration was abolished in 1852 and the Act repealed in 1905.

Irish militia reorganized; officer ranks were restricted to Protestants, but Catholics now permitted to join the other ranks.

Friendly Societies established by tradesmen to support members in hard times.

1794
A *Tour of Cambridgeshire*, the first of Charles Vancouver's reports for the Board of Agriculture is published. Further reports on Essex (1795), Devon (1808) and Hampshire

(1813) were published and contain invaluable detail for the counties and farming practices.

1795
Speenhamland system of poor relief introduced in some parts of the southern counties offering financial assistance linked to the price of bread.

Quota Acts were introduced which forced counties to supplement recruitment to the navy. Numbers provided varied from one part of the country to another – London had to provide an additional 5,700 men – but tens of thousands of men were required. Many petty criminals were used to make up the numbers. Indexed returns are kept in TNA and give the names and physical descriptions of men.

1795 (to 1869)
A tax of one guinea a year was levied on hair powder. Taxpayers received a certificate from the local Justice of the Peace. Some certificates can be found in local record offices (LRO) and give full names and position in a household.

1796
Trials in England of leading political radicals; many emigrate.

The Spinning Wheel Premium Entitlement List, or Flax Growers Bounty List, is an index of names of individuals across Ireland and in particular Ulster. It was drawn up in connection with a government initiative to encourage the linen trade by granting spinning wheels to those who planted flax on their land. The list is available online.

The Supplementary Militia Act raised an additional 64,000 men from across the country to serve in the war against France.

1795
Food riots and widespread famine in England after a poor harvest and high prices owing to war

1796
First vaccination by Edward Jenner against smallpox

1796 (to 1882)
A tax on the keeping of dogs; expressly limited to persons keeping sporting dogs or a number of dogs. (LRO)

1796 (to 1906)
Death Duties were introduced as a tax which was now liable on the estates left by a deceased person. Initially property transferred by legacy was taxed by way of a Legacy Duty. As the tax threshold was lowered in subsequent years more people were liable to pay. Indexed death duty registers (in TNA, with some early examples online) are often filled with detail that is of interest to the family historian.

1796 (to 1994)
Army records deaths of serving personnel. (TNA)

1797
Scottish militia was re-established by Act of Parliament.

1798
Income Tax introduced with further taxes between 1803-16 and 1842 to present!! ☹

1798 (to 1880)
A tax on Coats of Arms. All the nobility, old and new, were required to register their coats of arms, and pay for a licence to seal their letters with their arms.

1799
15,000 Irish militia joined the regular army in Britain.

Church Missionary Society founded.

1799 (to 1824)
The Combination Acts banned early trade unions.

1797
Battle of Fishguard (French invasion by 1400 troops)

1798
Uprising in Ireland – English militia volunteered for service in Ireland

Thomas Malthus publishes *An Essay on the Principle of Population*

1800s

1800
The Census (or Population) Act.

1801
Tuesday 10 March – National Census. Prompted in part by the panic caused by Malthus's predictions published in his *Essay on the Principles of Population*. Information was gathered parish by parish but no detail was collected on individual households. Local officials provided information on the number of inhabited and uninhabited houses in a parish, numbers of people who lived their, types of employment and numbers of baptisms, marriages and burials.

The first one-inch to one-mile map (of Kent) was published by the Ordnance Survey.

1803
Debrett's Peerage first published.

The Passenger Vessels Act was passed in order to regulate the transport of immigrants and emigrants and to ensure some level of safety. The act encouraged better sanitary arrangements on board ship and improvements in the provision of food and comfort. However, costs of emigration rose thus making it difficult for ordinary people to emigrate until the act was repealed in 1826.

1803
Naval pensions now paid via the Royal Naval Hospital Greenwich, London.

1803 (to 1804)
Parish constables drew up a list of men aged between 17 and 55 who might be called upon as a reserve force. Between 1803 and 1813, almost 100,000 militiamen joined the regular army.

1800
Formation of the United Kingdom by the Act of Union which incorporates Ireland

1801
Population 16.3 million

1801
Inclosure (Consolidation) Act

1801
(to 1804) Henry Addington, Tory

1802
One-year lull in hostilities between Britain and France

Factory Act

1803
(to 1815) War between Britain and France resumes; continual fear of invasion

1803
Lord Ellenborough's Act makes abortion a crime

1804
First railway steam locomotive

1804
(to 1806) William Pitt The Younger, Tory

Timeline (left column)

1805
Battle of Trafalgar

1806 (to 1809)
Lord Grenville,
William Grenville,
Tory

1806
Napoleon attempts an economic blockade of Britain

1807 (to 1809)
Duke of Portland,
William Bentinck,
Whig

1808 (to 1814)
British Army involved in the Peninsular Campaign in Spain

1809 (to 1812)
Spencer Perceval, Tory

1811
The Prince of Wales became Regent

1811
Population 18.5 million

1811 (to 1812)
First occurrence of Luddite activity in Nottingham

1812
Framebreaking Act imposes the death penalty for Luddites

1812 (to 1827)
Earl of Liverpool, Robert Jenkinson, Tory

1805

A database exists naming all the servicemen who participated in the Battle of Trafalgar. (Online via TNA)

1807

The import and use of slaves in Britain was outlawed though slavery continued in the colonies.

1808

County Asylums Act was passed, designed to encourage the construction of private asylums for the mentally ill. The first asylum opened in Northampton in 1811.

1811

Monday 27 May. A national census held which followed the format used ten years earlier. Enumerators were now asked to explain why houses were uninhabited in order that the prosperity of a given district could be judged more accurately.

The first national school for promoting religious education opens, providing basic tuition based on the teachings of the Church of England for the very poor. The schools, which were usually located near the parish church, were later absorbed into the state system.

1811 (to 1820)

Further Highland Clearances.

1812

England and Wales – Rose's Act. Ready printed forms for parish baptism and burial records. Baptism records contain: name of child, mother's name (not maiden name), father's name; occupation and residence, date of baptism, name of clergyman. Burial records contain: name, age, residence, date of burial and clergyman. The act came into force on 1 January 1813.

1812 (continued)
Some 250 regiments of local militia existed with more than 200,000 men enrolled.

Slave registers were introduced on plantations in the British Caribbean. The registers were discontinued after the abolition of slavery.

1814
James Pigot began publishing national directories, which are useful for the information they provide on professional people, nobles, gentry and clergy, coach and carrier services.

Navy Lists begin recording officers' names; published quarterly.

1815
The Battle of Waterloo which saw the final defeat of Napoleon, was the first campaign where the soldiers who had participated were issued with special medals. The names of soldiers are recorded in medal rolls.

1816
Large-scale emigration to North America from Ireland as 6,000 left, followed by a similar number the following year.

1817
Johnstone's London Directory printed.

1817 (until 1830)
The Greenwood brothers published a series of large-scale folding maps of most English counties. Exceptions were: Bucks, Cambs, Herefordshire, Herts, Norfolk, Oxon and Rutland.

1818 (to 1994)
The army begins to record marriages of serving personnel.

1814
(and 1816)
Further outbreaks of Luddism

1815
Corn Laws passed by Parliament

1816
'The year without a summer'

1816
(to 1826)
10,000 British troops based in India died during the first cholera pandemic

1818
The first well-documented ragged school, designed to benefit the poor, opened in Portsmouth.

1820
Publication of county directories begins which continues until the early 20th century.

First Europeans, including British, begin to settle in New Zealand.

1821
Monday 28 May. A national census was held following the format used in 1801 and 1811. Enumerators were now required to enquire about age in order that the government might establish how many men would be available to bear arms if necessary. The question was also designed to help improve the tables on which life assurance was based.

First census held in Ireland. All census records for the period 1821-1891 later destroyed.

1822
Between 15 September 1822 and 26 March 1823, some evidence of age was necessary when application was made for a license to marry. Usually a baptismal certificate was supplied. The change was, however, short-lived and was abandoned.

1823
The residential requirement for marriage whereby either the bride or groom had to have been resident in a parish for four weeks was reduced to fifteen days.

The first Mechanics' Institute opened in London – and in Ipswich and Manchester the following year – offering educational opportunities to adult workers. Hundreds more would open across the country.

1819
Peterloo Massacre

Singapore becomes a new trading post

1820
(to 1830)
George IV

1821
Population 20.9 million

1820s
Temperance societies begin in Scotland and Ulster, soon spreading to other parts of the UK

1822
George IV's celebrated visit to Edinburgh promoted national identity – including the adoption of tartan by clans

1823 (to 1837)
Tithe Applotment books begin in Ireland listing landholders including tenant farmers and lessees.

1824
The Combination Acts were repealed enabling workers to establish trade unions.

Quarterly prison returns, from 1824 to 1876, record the offence, date, place of conviction and term of sentence.

In Scotland, the probate of testaments was transferred to county Sheriff Courts.

1826
Establishment of London University as a secular alternative to Oxford and Cambridge Universities. Records of alumni have been published.

White's first commercial directory published for Hull; listing trades peoples' names and addresses.

Burke's Landed Gentry (originally called *Burke's Commoners*) and *Burke's Peerage, Baronetage and Knightage* were published by John Burke after years of genealogical research by members of his family. Revised editions have been published down the years until 1972.

1827
Greenwood's *Map of London* published.

1828
Test and Corporation Act repealed now permitting Catholics and Dissenters to hold public office.

1828 (to 1861)
Perry's *Bankrupt and Insolvent Gazette* published monthly.

1824
Society for the Prevention of Cruelty to Animals established

1825
Stockton and Darlington Railway opens - the first public steam railway in the world

1827
Publication of *The Shepherd's Calendar* by John Clare, a poetical account of the contemporary farming year

Burke and Hare start murdering

1827 (to 1827)
George Canning, Tory

1827 (to 1827)
Viscount Goderich, Frederick Robinson, Tory

1828
An Act to Regulate the Carrying of Passengers in Merchant Vessels passed to regulate safety for emigrants to the colonies

1828 (to 1830)
Duke of Wellington, Arthur Wellesley, Tory

1829
The first 'bobbies' appointed by Sir Robert Peel

Stephenson's Rocket wins the Rainhill Trials

1829
Ireland – in theory all Catholic baptisms, marriages and deaths to be recorded at parish level.

The Catholic Emancipation Act removed penalties against Catholics and culminated in the building of many Catholic churches and the return of monasticism in England.

1830s
A steep rise in the numbers of people who left Britain for good, in particular those who had been affected by agricultural depression. Many sailed from the port at Liverpool.

1830
Beer Act led to free trade in the brewing industry

1830
(to 1834)
Earl Grey, Charles Grey, Whig

1830
(to 1837)
William IV

1830
The Liverpool and Manchester Railway opens

Revolution in France and riots across Europe

Swing Riots in southern England

Bus mania in London as horse-drawn omnibuses proliferated

The Royal Geographical Society was formed in London

1830
Mormonism has its origins in the Church of Christ founded by Joseph Smith on 6 April in New York. Mormon belief in baptism for the dead has given rise to their interest in and support of genealogy.

The Plymouth Brethren, whose origins can be traced to Dublin about 1827, established at a meeting in Plymouth. In 1849 they split into Open Brethren and the Exclusive Brethren.

Cobbett's detailed account of the English countryside is published as *Rural Rides*.

Responsibility for divorce cases in Scotland transfers to the Court of Sessions.

1831
Sunderland – the first occurrence of cholera in Britain

Population 24.1 million

1831
Sunday 29 May – National Census. Enumerators were now required to ask about occupations. Only Londonderry returns survive for Ireland.

A list of all parish registers pre-dating 1813 compiled.

1831 (to 1848-9)
Publication of Samuel Lewis's *Topographical Dictionary of England* providing detail on towns and villages across the country and arranged alphabetically by place.

1832
Electoral registers (poll books) are compiled for the first time naming qualified voters, residence, and ownership of property in a polling district.

Parliamentary Act to encourage establishment of private cemeteries.

The Great Reform Act was passed which brought significant change to the electoral system as 'rotten boroughs' were abolished. The number of those eligible to vote increased to about one million men, although qualification was still largely based on property values. Electoral registers were introduced, listing qualified voters, residence and the basis of voting entitlement. The registers were compiled annually except between 1916-17 and 1940-44.

1833
The abolition of slavery occurred in the British Colonies. England frees 780,993 slaves throughout its colonies. Canada, as part of the British Empire, became a destination for American slaves escaping on the 'Underground Railroad'.

1833 (also 1846)
Samuel Lewis's *Topographical Dictionary of Wales* followed the format of the dictionary of England and included detailed maps.

1834
The Poor Law Amendment Act saw parishes grouped together as Poor Law Unions and the construction of more than 300

1831
(to 1832)
Collapse of the November Uprising leads to the first major influx of Polish people

1832
Approximately 55,000 people died of cholera

1832
(to 1833)
Beginnings of the Oxford Movement

1833
Charles Babbage designs the Difference Machine – a forerunner of the modern computer

1833
A Factory Act attempted to regulate working hours in the textile industry

1834
The Tolpuddle Martyrs

1834
(to 1834)
Viscount Melbourne, William Lamb, Whig

1834
(to 1834)
Duke of Wellington, Arthur Wellesley, Tory

1834
(to 1835)
Sir Robert Peel, Tory

1835
Mount St Bernard established; first Catholic monastery built in Britain since the Reformation

1835
(to 1841)
Viscount Melbourne, William Lamb, Whig

1835
The first photographic negatives exposed by Fox-Talbot

Christmas now a national holiday

London City Mission founded

1836
Irish Constabulary Act provides central organisation for the police in Ireland

1837
(to 1901)
Victoria

1837
Euston opens as the first London railway station

workhouses over the next five years. Few, if any, bastardy orders now made.

1835

The Marriage Act forbad marriages between closely related individuals in particular a man and his dead wife's sister (see 1907). Some married abroad to evade the law.

Local election poll books begin, consisting of those who had voted. They were not generally compiled for local elections.

The Municipal Corporations Act (or Municipal Reform Act) reformed local government in 178 incorporated boroughs in England and Wales. Unincorporated towns such as Birmingham could now request incorporation. The councils in such towns, were now to be elected by men who had paid rates for at least three years. The names of these rate-payers (or burgesses) were recorded in rate books.

The Merchant Shipping Act – all crew lists to be logged.

1836

The Tithe Commutation Act abolished the ancient system of paying tithes in goods. Fixed charges were introduced – ending in 1936. Tithe maps, of which some 12,000 survive, were prepared across the country in 1840 that give names of owners and occupiers of land.

The General Register Office for England and Wales established with a Registrar General.

1837

1 July – Civil registration of Birth, Marriages and Deaths (BMD) begins in England and Wales. It was now possible for a marriage to be performed in a certified building other than a church.

1837 (continued)

Samuel *Lewis's Topographical Dictionary of Ireland* published providing a highly detailed description of towns and villages in Ireland and is an important account of Ireland before the Great Famine.

The Wills Act raised the legal age for writing a will to 21 years. Nuncupative wills (made by word of mouth on a deathbed) were now only valid for members of the armed forces who died in action.

1837 (and 1838)

Burke's Commoners of Great Britain and Ireland contains information about people who owned land or held high official rank but were not considered nobility.

1838

The Public Record Office established in Chancery Lane.

Irish Poor Law Act established a system of workhouses and a Poor Rate levy to pay for them.

1840

The Outdoor Relief Prohibitory Order restricted assistance given to the poor outside the workhouse.

Civil registration begins in Guernsey.

1841

Sunday 6 June – National Census. First national census to record more detailed information and is the earliest census generally used by family historians. Full name, sex, and age of those under 16 years of age was given exactly, but those over 16 were rounded down to the nearest unit of 5. Enumerators also recorded the occupation of people living in a household. Many seasonal

1838
Massive Chartist Demonstrations

Outbreaks of smallpox kill tens of thousands (until 1841)

Samuel Morse demonstrates the telegraph

1839
(to 1844) Rural protests called the Rebecca Riots in Wales

1839
County Police Act allowing voluntary establishment of rural forces (see also 1856)

1840
Height of railway mania

Introduction of the Penny Black

1841
The first excursion by rail organised by Thomas Cook

Population 26.8 million

1841
(to 1846) Sir Robert Peel, Tory

workers not included. Only the returns for Cavan survive for Ireland.

1842

Civil registration begins in Jersey.

First edition of *The Illustrated London News*, the first illustrated weekly newspaper. It included all kinds of topical news (British and foreign) including stories about crime and social issues. The newspaper also carried details of births, marriages and deaths and advertisements. It was published weekly until 1971 and then less frequently until its closure in 2003. An archive is available online.

British Mines Act outlawed employment of women and girls in mines.

Military pensions were now paid through local offices instead of the Royal Hospitals.

1844

The Naturalisation Act – procedure for naturalisation was simplified.

The Companies Act required registration of all companies.

Factories Act restricted hours of work for women and children.

Friedrich Engels publishes *The Condition of the Working Class in England* based on his observations in Manchester.

1845

Kelly's Directories begin which supplement the information given in other directories with lists of some individuals.

The Lunacy and County Asylum Acts were passed describing those with mental illness as patients. Officials were given the task of establishing and inspecting asylums. Many mentally ill individuals incarcerated in

---

1842
Britain gains Hong Kong

1844
Bank Charter Act allows only the Bank of England to issue banknotes

Railways Act extended rail travel, 200,000 navvies were employed to construct lines across the country, all the main lines complete by 1852

1845
General Enclosure Act

1845
The Great Hunger (famine) in Ireland. Two million Irish emigrate to US over next 10 years.

Collapse of bridge in Great Yarmouth kills 80

workhouses were removed to asylums.

Ireland lost 16% of its population between 1845 and the end of famine in 1852.

The first Medical Directory is published with names, addresses, qualifications and other details on general practitioners.

A Scottish Poor Law Act established Parochial Boards under the direction of the central Board of Supervision to collect and distribute funds to those in need of support and unable to work. Poor houses could be set up at the discretion of the Boards in large parishes or groups of parishes.

Civil registration of non-Catholic marriages begins in Ireland.

1846
Samuel Lewis's *Topographical Dictionaries of Scotland and of Wales* published.

1847
The Consolidated General Order was instituted regulating life in workhouses across the country.

1847 (to1865)
Griffith's Valuation Lists record every land and householder in Ireland, with a description of their property.

1847 (to 1886)
Assisted emigration to Australia begins. Some (but not all) passenger lists survive and some have been made available online.

1849
Civil registration of births and marriages begins on the Isle of Man but was voluntary.

First edition of the quarterly *Notes and Queries*, which contains much of

1846 Very hot summer gives rise to many epidemics	**1846** (to 1852) Lord John Russell, Whig
1847 A typhus epidemic kills more than 30,000	
1848 Year of Revolutions in Europe	**1848** Public Health Act
Californian Gold Rush begins	
Karl Marx and Fredrick Engels publish *The Communist Manifesto*	
1848 (to 1850) A cholera epidemic claimed 52,000 lives	

genealogical interest. An archive is available online.

The first edition of *Who's Who*, was published, a compilation of biographies of prominent Britons. It has been published annually since its inception.

1850

Civil registration begins on Alderney.

1851

Sunday 30 March. A national census in which more detailed information was recorded namely the relationship of each individual to the head of the household and whether any individual was deaf or blind. Information on the place of birth was also recorded. This census was the first to record the numbers of persons living on vessels in inland waters or at sea, those serving abroad (with the armed forces or with the East India Company) and also those resident overseas. For Ireland only the returns for Fermanagh and Antrim survive.

The 'Religious Census' was held on 30 March amid much controversy. All places of worship across England, Wales and Scotland were recorded with a view to finding out the extent of religious instruction. Although reports, made by ministers, were not compulsory, thousands were returned. The Scottish report lacked detail but the report for England and Wales was full of information and was published in 1854.

1851 (to 1924)
A new tax called the Empty House Tax (or simply House Duty) was imposed after the repeal of the Window Tax.

1852
Civil registration districts re-organised.

1852 (continued)
A Burials Act permitted local authorities to open cemeteries to relieve the overcrowding of churchyards.

1853
A Succession Duty was introduced in connection with death duties as tax was now payable on the legal transfer of a dead person's assets.

1853 (to 1923)
Records for Naval Ratings begin giving details of birth, physical appearance, occupation and ships upon which they served. (TNA)

1853 (until 1948)
Vaccination against smallpox, administered through workhouses, was now compulsory. Registers of those vaccinated were kept from 1862.

1854 (to 1975)
The Lands Valuation (Scotland) Act established assessors offices in each Scottish county and royal burgh whose task it was to produce lists of properties above a certain value. The returns which were often very detailed with information for example on tenants or other occupiers, have been digitised and are available online via NAS.

1855
Civil Registration begins in Scotland.

Many regional newspapers founded as stamp duty on newspapers is abolished.

Smallpox vaccination now compulsory – records survive from 1862 though rarely offer any personal details.

1852
(to 1855)
Earl of Aberdeen, George Hamilton-Gordon, Conservative

1853
(to 1854)
London cholera epidemic kills more than 10,000 people

1854
(to 1856)
Crimean War

The Charge of the Light Brigade

1855
(to 1858)
Viscount Palmerston, Henry Temple, Liberal

1856
Van Diemen's Land re-named Tasmania

1856
County and Borough Police Act - compulsory establishment of county forces

1857
Indian revolt

First Victoria Cross awarded

1857
The Court of Probate Act moved responsibility for the granting of probate and letters of administration from the church courts to a new civil court and created the Principal Probate registry in London and several district probate registries.

The Matrimonial Causes Act permitted divorce in England and Wales on grounds of adultery by the wife or in some cases, of adultery by the husband. The Act gave women who were living apart from their husbands, control over money from bequests and investments and other earnings. It came into force on 1 January 1858 except in Ireland where a private parliamentary act was required. Jurisdiction over matrimonial issues passed from church to civil courts.

1858
(to 1859) Earl of Derby, Edward Stanley, Conservative

1858
The Great Stink in London gave rise to the construction of the sewers

Charles Darwin publishes *Origin of Species*

First case of diphtheria recorded

1858
English, Welsh and Irish wills, previously proved by ecclesiastical courts, were now granted by civil probate registries in London and Dublin. Wills and administrations, granted by local probate officers, were indexed separately.

Crockford's Clerical Directory begins containing brief biographical details of Anglican clergy in Britain.

1859
(to 1865) Viscount Palmerston, Henry Temple, Liberal

1859
Diphtheria epidemic

The Anglesey Ship Disaster

1859
Medical registers begin.

1860
Francis Frith begins his project to photograph every town and village across Britain.

1861
Prince Albert dies of typhus

1861
Population 29 million

1861
(to 1865) American Civil War

1861
Sunday 7 April. National census using the format that had been adopted in 1851.

American Civil War led to blockade of cotton exports with devastating effect on the English textile industry leading to riots in spring 1863.

1862
The Land Registry Act was passed in an effort to record the conveyance of land in the UK. Further acts in 1875 and 1897 improved the system until it was overhauled in 1925.

1864
Civil registration of all births, marriages and deaths begins in Ireland.

1865
The Salvation Army, was founded by William and Catherine Booth as the East London Christian Mission. It was founded in Wales in 1874 and in Jersey and Scotland in 1879.

William Lawrence begins his project to photograph the towns and villages of Ireland. The complete collection is available online.

Record of Title Act was passed for Ireland to regulate the recording of land conveyance. The records, can be accessed by the public for a small fee.

1866
Age of the deceased now added to death index.

Agricultural Returns begin to be collected. Later called Parish Summaries. A few late 18th and early 19th century returns were made; all originals have been destroyed but copies can be found in TNA.

1867
Second Reform Act enfranchised the male town dwellers and widened eligibility amongst men who lived in rural areas in England and Wales doubling the numbers entitled to vote to about two million. A similar act passed in Scotland the following year doubled the number of voters to about 230,000.

1863
London Underground opens

1863
Public Works Act

1864
The Sheffield Flood left 270 dead

1865
(to 1866)
Earl Russell, John Russell, Liberal

1860s
Mechanised mower and reapers begin to replace the traditional sickle and scythe

1866
In London's East End, a cholera epidemic killed 5,500

Oaks Colliery disaster

1866
(to 1868)
Earl of Derby, Edward Stanley, Conservative

1867
Fenian rising in Ireland

1867 (continued)

The Agricultural Gangs Act (covering England and Wales) was passed to regulate the employment of women and children and to ensure that gang masters were licensed.

The discovery of diamonds in central South Africa led to the departure of many Britons.

1868

In Scotland the age at death was added to death index.

It was now possible to stipulate inheritance of real estate in a will. Previously this was governed by strict rules of descent.

Transportation of convicts to Australia ends.

Collection of church rates abolished by an act of parliament.

1869

Female rate-payers (single or widowed) could now vote in municipal elections, for Poor Law boards and (from 1870) for school boards. The qualifying residency period for all municipal voters was reduced to one year.

The completion of the Suez Canal led to a strong British presence in Egypt, Sudan and East Africa.

1869 (to 1948)

The Lloyd's Captains' Registers begin recording details of careers. They are held in the London Metropolitan Archives.

1870s

Returns of Owners of Land were introduced for those with holdings of more than an acre; England in 1873, Scotland 1874 and Ireland 1876.

1868
(to 1868)
Benjamin Disraeli, Conservative

1868
(to 1874)
William Ewart Gladstone, Liberal

1869
Church of Ireland disestablished as the state church

The Debtor's Act ended imprisonment for debt

1868
Abolition of public executions

1869
Great Fire of Whitstable drew thousands of sightseers and devastated the town

1870

Married Women's Property Act (and another in 1882) gave married women the same rights over property as unmarried women.

Women now admitted into Oxford and Cambridge University.

Dr Barnardo opens his first home for orphaned children in Stepney, London.

Forster's Education Act provided elementary education for children of 5 to 12 years.

Teachers were required to keep attendance lists and log books of events on a weekly basis.

Gladstone introduced an Irish Land Act to reform injustices with regard to land ownership in Ireland. Further and more effective acts were passed in the 1880s.

In England and Wales, wills and probate administration were now indexed together.

1871

Sunday 2 April. A national census which continued the earlier format but to which a further question was added concerning whether any member of the household was an 'imbecile or idiot' or 'feeble-minded'. This question was not asked in 1911 and after. Individuals were also asked about their employment status

Trade Unions were now legalised.

Military pensions introduced.

1872

Parliamentary elections were now to be secret in Britain and Ireland. Prior to this poll books could show how a person voted. Poll books were now discontinued.

1870
Agricultural Depression began – land values drop and many bankruptcies amongst farmers

Horse-drawn trams introduced to London

1870
Army Enlistment (Short Service) Act allows for shorter service period

Naturalisation Act

1871
Bank Holidays introduced for bank workers and soon adopted more widely

Population 31.6 million

Guncotton factory explosion, Stowmarket

1871
Regulation of the Forces Act (Cardwell Reforms), creates a structure of regional Brigade (Regimental) Districts

1872
First ever FA Cup Final

1872 (until 1939)
Barnardo began to send children to Canada through Miss Annie Macpherson's organization.

1873
England and Wales - the Returns of the Owners of Land published - organised by county with landowners' addresses, land holdings and gross rental value.

1874
(to 1880)
Benjamin Disraeli, Conservative

1874
Massive storms along coast of north east England

1874
A Factory Act introduces a 56-hour week.

The Births and Deaths Registration Act made registration compulsory. Registration of a birth was now the responsibility of a baby's parents or the occupier of the house where a birth took place. Registration had to take place within 42 days else a fine of £2 was payable. The date of birth, was sometimes altered by parents who failed to register within the specified time limit.

The father of an illegitimate child could be recorded in the birth register if he accompanied the child's mother. So a child may be indexed twice under two different surnames. Mothers were however, permitted to register a father's name without his consent on a birth certificate.

Responsibility for recording a death now fell to a relative of the deceased. Registration had to be made within five days of death and the cause of death was now to be certified by a doctor before a certificate could be issued. Burial authorities now required official notification regarding the registration of a death in order to prevent unauthorised interment.

Stillborn babies were now to be registered by their parents.

1875

The Artisans and Labourers Dwellings Improvement Act passed allowing local councils to purchase, demolish and replace slum housing. In Birmingham, some slum areas were rebuilt though relatively few councils acted until later in the century.

Some Church of Ireland registers were now sent to the PRO in Dublin (marriage registers dating from before 1845 and baptisms and burial registers from 1871). About 60% were deposited.

1876

Annual centralised list of Scottish wills.

Ireland - the Returns of the Owners of Land published - organised by county with landowners' addresses, land holdings and gross rental value.

1878

Civil registration of births and deaths now compulsory on the Isle of Man.

Electoral registers now begin to show both Parliamentary and municipal voters as a result of a Registration Act.

A Factory and Workshop Act consolidated previous legislation and applied it to all trades. The minimum working age was raised to 10 years. Children below the age of 10 were required to attend school. Subsequent acts refined, amended and extended the provisions including raising the minimum employment age to 11 from 1891 and to 12 in 1901.

1879

The Irish Land League was established, as a political organization set up to help poor tenant farmers find ways of owning the land they worked.

1875
The Public Health Act enabled local authorities to make bye-laws regulating the building of new housing

1876
Alexander Graham Bell patents the telephone

1876
Royal Titles Act – Queen Victoria to be proclaimed Empress of India

1878
The SS Princess Alice disaster

1879
Anglo-Zulu War

A public telephone service begins in Britain

Tay Bridge disaster

1880

The Elementary Education Act now made schooling compulsory for children from 5-10 years of age. Children of 13 years and under who were in work, had to have a certificate to demonstrate that they had reached a certain standard.

The Burials Laws Amendment Act permitted the interment of any who were entitled to burial in a parochial burial place provided the church incumbent was informed. A religious service was no longer required. The Act also permitted the use of a Church of England service on unconsecrated ground.

First British telephone directory published.

1881

Sunday 3 April. A national census using the pattern established in 1871. In Scotland, enumerators were required to ask if Gaelic was spoken at home.

Army regiments change to territorial titles.

1882

The Married Womens' Property Act provided women in England, Wales and Ireland the same rights as single women with regard to managing their finances. This extended women some say in owning property, running businesses and other financial matters. Scottish acts passed in 1877, 1880 and 1881 similarly improved womens' rights in controlling their finances and property.

1884

Civil Registration for marriages on the Isle of Man now compulsory. Probate was transferred from church courts to the Manx High Court of Justice.

The Third Reform Act gives the vote to most male householders in rural areas.

1880
Greenwich Mean Time (GMT) adopted across Great Britain

1880
The University of London awards the first degrees to women

1880
(to 1885)
William Ewart Gladstone, Liberal

1880
(to 1881)
First Anglo-Boer War

1881
(to 1884)
Anti-Jewish pogroms in Russia – thousands flee; some settling in England

Population 35 million

1882
Militant Irish Republicans kill Lord Frederick Cavendish and Thomas Henry Burke in Phoenix Park, Dublin

1883
Sunderland Theatre Disaster

Boys Brigade founded

1884
The Fabian Society is founded in London

1884
(to 1885)
Berlin Conference divides Africa among European colonial powers

1884 (to 1943)
Reports of suitability of naval officers for promotion.

1885
The cremation of the dead was legalized and the first crematorium in Britain opened in Woking, Surrey.

The Salvation Army established a Family Tracing Service by which it attempts to reunite family members.

1888
A Local Government Act established county councils and boroughs in England and Wales; effective early 1889, abolished 1974. A similar Scottish Act came into force in 1880.

County Electors Act was introduced so that now individuals who paid rates or occupied property with a rental value of more than £10 qualified for the vote in county and borough elections. Women qualified on the same basis if they were rate-payers or occupiers in their own right.

1889
Charles Booth begins his detailed survey of the London poor which is available online. The survey was made, by Booth and his assistants walking the London streets and reporting on the state of housing and living conditions in each one. Booth produced a map to accompany the report.

1891
Sunday 5 April. A national census was held which made use of the established format though the question regarding employment status was removed until 1931. Instead, individuals were asked if they were an employer or employee. In Wales,

Mid-1880s
Gold rush in central South Africa

1888
The first Kodak cameras on sale

Jack the Ripper

The National Geographic Society was formed

1889
First moving pictures developed on celluloid film

1891
The Great Blizzard

Population 37.8 million

1885
(to 1886)
Marquess of Salisbury, Robert A T Gascoyne-Cecil, Conservative

1886
(to 1887)
William Ewart Gladstone, Liberal

1887
(to 1892)
Marquess of Salisbury, Robert A T Gascoyne-Cecil, Conservative

1889
Prevention of Cruelty to, and Protection of, Children Act

1889
First Official Secrets Act

enumerators asked individuals what languages were spoken in the home.

1892
The Foreign Marriage Act granted validation to certain marriages that occurred abroad where one of the parties was a British subject.

1893

1893
Independent Labour Party founded in Bradford

Elementary Education (School Attendance) Act raised the school leaving age to 11 and later to 13 years of age. A further act made education compulsory for children who were deaf or blind. Provision was made for special schools to be established.

1894

1894
(to 1895) Earl of Rosebery, Liberal

Royal Mail permits publishers in Britain to make and distribute picture postcards.

Estate Duty was introduced whereby a tax was levied on assets owned by a person at death.

The Local Government Act established Urban and Rural District Councils and Parish Councils elected by rate payers.

1895

1895
(to 1902) Marquess of Salisbury, Robert A T Gascoyne-Cecil, Conservative

1896
Marconi invents the wireless telegraph – first used in England

Underground railway in Glasgow opens

Notification of infectious diseases became compulsory.

The *Dictionary of National Biography* first published.

1898
Non-conformist churches were now permitted to have a member of their congregation appointed as a registrar of marriages.

Catholic priests can now perform legally binding marriages.

1898 (continued)
Local Government Act (Ireland) formed county councils.

The value of total estate was now shown in the probate indexes of England and Wales.

1899
The very informative and illustrated *Victoria County History* series begins with detailed commentaries on each county and discussion of buildings of historical note and much of interest to the genealogist.

1900s

1900
Higher elementary schools were recognized providing education from the age of 10 to 15 years of age.

One in six of the population of England and Wales were employed 'in service'.

1901
Sunday 31 March. A national census held. A question was added to the established format, enquiring if individuals worked at home. Returns are complete for Ireland.

1902
Provision for secondary education through Balfour's Education Act.

1903
In Ireland, the mother's maiden name was now added to birth index.

1905
An Aliens' Act introduced registration of immigrants and restrictions on those who came to settle in Britain. The act was designed to prevent destitute individuals or criminals entering the country.

1899
(to 1902)
Second Anglo-Boer War

Losses during Black Week (10 to 17 December) resulted in recruitment of an additional 180,000 men

1900
Labour Party formed

1901
Marconi transmitted the first radio wave

Population 41.6 million

1901
House of Saxe-Coburg and Gotha

1901
(to 1910)
Edward VII

1902
(to 1905)
Arthur Balfour, Conservative

1903
Suffragettes formed

First aeroplane flight

1905
Albert Einstein publishes his theory of relativity

1905
(to 1908)
Sir Henry Campbell-Bannerman, Liberal

1906

Inheritance Tax introduced.

The Marriage with Foreigners Act meant that notice had to be given to a local superintendent registrar for some (but not all) marriages that took place abroad.

1907

Midwives (or parents of a child) were now required to notify the local health ministry of births to prevent missed registration.

The Deceased Wife's Sister's Marriage Act allowed a man to marry his dead wife's sister.

1908

The Children Act introduced regulations concerning baby farming and wet nursing and led to the establishment of juvenile courts and many orphanages.

1909

Old Age Pensions introduced by Lloyd George, helped to alleviate the fear of entering a workhouse.

1910 (to 1915)

A survey of land ownership in England and Wales, sometimes called Lloyd George's Doomsday, was carried out in support of The Finance Act.

1911

Sunday 2 April. A National Census known as the 'fertility census' was boycotted by the suffragist Womens' Freedom League. Irish returns complete.

The National Insurance Act gave sickness benefits to working people and access to a doctor.

Mothers' maiden names added to birth index.

1907
Scouts founded

1908
(to 1916)
Herbert H Asquith, Liberal
(1915 Coalition)

1909
Rail and coal strikes

Ellan Vannin paddle steamer disaster

1910
(to present)
House of Windsor

1910
Girl Guides founded

Westhoughton Pit Disaster

1910
(to 1936)
George V

1911
Sidney Street Siege

Population 42.1 million

1911 (continued)

The Society of Genealogists established.

Unemployment benefits introduced.

1912

A spouse's surname was added to the GRO marriage indexes in England and Wales.

1913

The first child migrants in modern times arrived in Western Australia, bound for the Fairbridge School at Pinjarra in Western Australia. As many as 130,000 children were subsequently taken to colonial outposts until the migrant scheme stopped in 1970.

1914

Notice of official name changes by deed poll now published in *The London Gazette*.

British Nationality and Status of Aliens Act – all aliens over 16 to register with police.

1915

Civil registration introduced on Sark.

National registration was introduced as a wartime measure and was administered by the General Registry Office.

1916 (to 1919)
Military Service Act – compulsory military conscription.

1918

The Representation of the People Act (or Fourth Reform Act) gave votes to men over 21 years of age and to women over 30 who were householders or wives of householders. The format of electoral registers also changed.

A parliamentary act made secondary education compulsory for all up to 14 years of age.

1912
RMS Titanic sinks

First cinema opens in Clevedon, Somerset

1913
Suffragette demonstrations in London

Caerphilly mining disaster

1914
First World War starts

Battle of Ypres

German raid on Scarborough and Hartlepool

1914
Irish Home Rule Act

1915
Gallipoli

Lusitania sunk

1916
Battle of Verdun

Battle of Jutland

Battle of the Somme

1916
(to 1922) David Lloyd George, Liberal (Coalition)

1917
Russian revolution

Battle of Passchendaele

USA enters war

1918
First World War ends

Armistice – 11 November

1918
The Royal Flying Corps and the Royal Naval Air Service are merged to form the Royal Air Force

1918
(to 1919) Flu Pandemic

1919 Treaty of Versailles	**1919** Britain adopts a 48-hour working week Sinking of HMS Iolaire off Stornoway
1920 Irish Free State Established	
1921 Irish Treaty	**1921** Population 44 million
1922 (to 1923) Andrew Bonar Law, Conservative	**1922** British Broadcasting Corporation established First public radio broadcasts in the UK
1923 (to 1924) Stanley Baldwin, Conservative	**1923** Founding of the English Place-Name Society

1919
Soldiers discharged from WW1 service.

1920s
British control of East African region strengthens with significant colonial settlement until 1939.

1920
Census Act provided for a mid-term census and importantly included a statutory 100 year prohibition on disclosure.

Oxford University admit women to degrees.

1921
Sunday 19 June. National Census.

1922
A sustained IRA attack on the Four Courts in Dublin, which housed the GRO and the PRO, at the end of June resulted in the destruction of many Protestant parish records, most poll books, wills, and almost all census returns from 1821-51. Complete census returns survive for 1901 and 1911 and a few fragments for 1821, 1831, 1841 and 1851. Census returns from 1861-91 had been pulped during WW1. The indexes for pre-1858 wills and the copies of will transcripts made thereafter and held in other places, were not affected.

The BMD registers for Northern Ireland and the Republic of Ireland were now kept separately.

The Law of Property Act brought an end to the manorial system with the final change of copyhold to freehold land taking place in 1926.

1923
Women now have the same rights in divorce as men if adultery could be proved.

1923 (until 1967)
The first Barnardo's child migrants arrived in New South Wales, Australia.

1924
The Big Brother Movement founded to encourage young Britons to emigrate to Australia.

1925
The Land Registration Act introduced a system which remains in use.

1926
Births and Deaths Registration Act introduced the need for a legal proof (registrar's certificate or coroner's order) before a burial or cremation could take place. Notice also had to be made to a registrar once a funeral had occurred.

The act also made the registration of stillborn babies mandatory (in order to counteract infanticide). This took effect from 1 July 1927 though no national indexes are available.

A widow's entitlement to an intestate husband's estate increased from one third to one half. The remainder was to pass to children.

Adoption of Children Act – adoption of children legalised by parliamentary act – came into effect January 1927.

The Legitimacy Act permitted offspring of unmarried parents to be legitimised provided the parents had been free to marry when their child was born.

1928
Women over 21 years of age now get the vote.

1924
(to 1924)
James Ramsey MacDonald, Labour

1924
(to 1929)
Stanley Baldwin, Conservative

1925
John Logie Baird demonstrates television publicly

1926
General Strike

1927
BBC founded under Royal Charter

1928
Alexander Fleming notices penicillin – the revolution of antibiotics is started

Timeline (left column)

1929
(to 1935)
Ramsay MacDonald, Labour

1935
(to 1937)
Stanley Baldwin, Conservative

1936
(January to December)
Edward VIII

1936
(to 1952)
George VI

1937
(to 1940)
Neville Chamberlain, Conservative

Events (second column)

1929
Worldwide economic depression leads to mass unemployment and poverty

1930
One fifth of the British male workforce were unemployed

Clyde Tombaugh discovers Pluto

1931
Population 46 million

1932
Great Hunger March

1934
Gresford Pit Disaster

1936
Spanish Civil War begins

Battle of Cable Street, London

1929

The age of consent (the minimum age for marriage to take place) was raised to 16 with parental consent by the Act of Marriage Act. It was previously variable though generally held at 14 for boys and 12 for girls.

In Scotland, a mother's maiden name was added to the birth index.

Workhouses were abolished under the Local Government Act of 1929.

1931

Sunday 26 April. National Census. A question regarding employment status was re-introduced. All records for the 1931 census in England and Wales were destroyed in an accidental fire at Hayes, in Middlesex in 1942.

1933

Refugees from Nazi Germany begin to arrive: some in transit for the US; many settle in UK.

1937

4,000 Basque children brought to England to escape danger.

Matrimonial Causes Act broadened grounds of divorce, extended to Northern Ireland in 1939.

1938

Population Act allows for the collation of birth registrations.

Arrival of the first Kindertransport as young Jewish children were evacuated from Germany. The scheme continued until the outbreak of war in September 1939. 10,000 children were brought to safety. Many stayed permanently.

1939
Friday 29 September. A mini census so that everyone could be issued with an identity card.

Evacuation of women and children from London begins.

1939 (to 1960)
Compulsory military National Service. Formalised by the National Service Act 1948.

1940
September to May 1941 – the Blitz resulted in thousands of civilian deaths and destruction of records, including military records.

1941
National Census – no census was held in 1941 because of the Second World War.

America joined the war and there were thousands of liaisons between US servicemen and British women. As many as 100,000 'GI babies' were born and as many marriages took place as women went to America after the war.

1942
Exeter bombed with the loss of almost all pre-1858 wills for Somerset, Devon and Cornwall. Some pre-existing abstracts and copies survive.

1944
The Education (or Butler) Act established the tripartite education system of grammar schools, secondary modern schools and secondary technical schools.

1945
The NRA established to collect information about manuscripts outside public records.

1939
Britain (and France) declare war on Germany – start of World War Two

Evacuation known as Operation Pied Piper

1940
Dunkirk evacuations

Battle of Britain

1940
(to 1945)
Winston Churchill, Conservative

1941
Population 48.2 million

Blitz over Swansea

Special Air Service formed

First Canadian soldiers arrive in UK

1942
Battle of El Alamein

First American soldiers arrive in the UK

1943
Dam Buster raids

1944
D-Day landings

1945
8 May – Victory in Europe Day

1945
(to 1951)
Clement Attlee, Labour

1945

15 August –
Victory in Japan
Day

George Orwell;
Animal Farm

1947

Very harsh winter

Education was
now compulsory
to 15 years of age

1948

National Health
Service begins

Summer
Olympics
in London

Railways
nationalised

1951

(to 1955)
Winston Churchill,
Conservative

1951

Population
50.2 million

1945 (to 1972)
The Australian government began to encourage British citizens to emigrate under an assisted passage scheme.

1946
Family Census carried out by the Registrar General on behalf of the Royal Commission on Population.

Civil registration districts reorganised.

1947
Polish Resettlement Act offered citizenship to over 200,000 displaced Polish troops in Britain.

1948
The British Nationality Act created the new status of Citizen of the United Kingdom and the Colonies. All Commonwealth citizens now qualified for British passports. Thereafter many thousands came to Britain in search of work.

The Poor Law abolished by parliamentary act.

1949
In Guernsey, married womens' deaths were now recorded under the married name. Previously the record had been under the maiden name.

In Jersey probate jurisdiction was transferred from the Ecclesiastical Court of the Dean Jersey to the Principal Probate Registry in London.

1951
Sunday 8 April. National Census.

1951 (to 1953)
British troops were involved in the Korean War. Almost 700 would die; more than 1,000 were prisoners of war.

1951 (to 1974)
The first of Nikolaus Pevsner's *The Buildings of England* is published – detailed surveys of all buildings of historical note across the country.

1952
February – national identity cards abolished.

1957
The 'Bring out a Briton' scheme was initiated to encourage further migration from Britain to Australia.

1958
Public Records Act – 50 year rule, amended 1967.

1960
The Population Statistics Act required the compulsory notification of causes of stillbirths.

1961
Sunday 23 April. National Census.

1962
Commonwealth Immigrants Act increased the residence period for Commonwealth citizens (plus British subjects and Irish citizens) applying for registration as citizens of the UK and its Colonies from one year to five years thus making it harder to gain permanent status.

1966
A mini-census was held on 24 April, based on a 10% sample of the population.

1967
A Public Record Act shortens length of time records closed to 30 years, except for census records which remain closed for 100 years. Further redefined by the Freedom of Information Act in 2000.

1952 Great Smog of London kills many	**1952** (to present) **Elizabeth II**
1953 Severe storms and high tides led to many deaths	
Hillary and Tenzing climb Mount Everest	
	1955 (to 1957) Sir Anthony Eden, Conservative
1956 Hungarian revolution (refugees come to Britain)	
1957 Publication of the Wolfenden report on homosexuality and prostitution	**1957** (to 1963) Harold Macmillan, Conservative
Windscale disaster	
1959 Auchengeich pit disaster	
1961 First man in space	
Population 52.8 million	
1962/3 The Big Freeze	**1963** (to 1964) Sir Alec Douglas-Home, Conservative
1965 Abolition of capital punishment	**1964** (to 1970) Harold Wilson, Labour
Race Relations Act	
National Survey of Gypsies	
1966 The Troubles begin in Northern Ireland	
Aberfan disaster: 'a generation wiped out'	
1968 Severe floods across England	

1969
First man lands
on the moon

1969

The format of birth and death registers and certificates changed. Spaces were now made for a child's surname and parents' place of birth.

A Divorce Reform Act passed, came into effect in 1971, making it easier to divorce.

The Family Law Reform Act enabled illegitimate offspring to inherit if either parent died intestate.

In Scotland, England and Wales, the date of birth was added to death index.

1970
(to 1974)
Edward Heath,
Conservative

The age at majority was reduced from 21 to 18 years of age.

Some 80,000 Britons emigrated to Australia.

1971
Decimalisation

Courts Act

Population
55.9 million

Ibrox Stadium
disaster

1971

Sunday 25 April. National Census.

Immigration Act permitted individual right of abode in the UK if they, their husband, parents or grandparents had a connection with the UK, Channel Islands or the Isle of Man.

1971 (to present)
Electoral Register (eligibility to vote) – now available for all men and women over the age of 18.

1972
Bloody Sunday

1972

55,000 Ugandans of Asian origin are forced to flee and settle in Britain, many coming to towns in the Midlands.

Formation of United Reformed Church.

The newly created OPCS absorbs the GRO.

1973
Britain and
Ireland join EEC

1973
Concorde crosses
the Atlantic

1973

Fire at the National Personnel Records

Center in America destroys 16-18 million military personnel files – relevant to World War Two 'GI babies'.

Burghs in Scotland replaced by regions and districts.

1974
Local Government Act (England and Wales) transformed the county structure as boundaries were changed. Some counties ceased to exist and new ones came into being. 179 registration districts were abolished and many others were re-named.

A mother's maiden name was added to the Scottish GRO death indexes.

1975
The Children Act permitted an adopted person to apply for their birth certificate.

The Capital Transfer tax replaced previous death duty taxes.

1976
Deaths exceeded live births in England and Wales for the first time since records began in 1837.

1977
The National Archives opened in Kew as an adjunct to the PRO.

The Abandoned Childrens' Register was introduced to record all babies whose parents were not known. Previously details were recorded at parish level.

1981
Sunday 5 April. National census.

British Nationality Act abolished the status of the Citizens of UK and Colonies Act.

1974 Flixborough chemical plant explosion	**1974** (to 1976) Harold Wilson, Labour
	1975 Equal Pay Act and Sex Discrimination Act
	1976 (to 1979) James Callaghan, Labour
1979 SAS storm Iranian Embassy	**1979** Lord Mountbatten killed
	1979 (to 1990) Margaret Thatcher, Conservative
1981 Riots across Britain	
Population 56.3 million	
1982 Falklands War	

Timeline

1984
(to 1985)
Miners' Strike

1985
Toxteth and Broadwater Farm riots

Bradford City Stadium Fire

1987
The Great Storm

1988
Lockerbie

1989
Piper Alpha oil rig disaster

Kegworth air disaster

Hillsborough Stadium disaster

Marchioness riverboat disaster

1990
(to 1997)
John Major, Conservative

1990
Poll Tax riots

1990
(to 1991)
Gulf War One

1991
Population 57.8million

1993
Establishment of European Union

1994
First women priests ordained in the Church of England

1994
Channel Tunnel opens

1997
Diana, Princess of Wales died

1997
(to 2007)
Tony Blair, Labour

1984
In England and Wales the GRO BMD registers were now arranged annually instead of quarterly.

1987
The distinction between illegitimacy and legitimacy lifted by parliamentary act.

1988
An Education Reform Act made wide-ranging changes, including the notion of competition whereby schools were encouraged to compete for pupils.

1990
A Poll Tax, or community charge, replaced domestic rates.

1991
Sunday 21 April. National census. As many as one million uncounted owing to fears that the government would use information to enforce a poll tax.

1994
Council areas replace regions and districts in Scotland.

1995
From 1 April any suitable privately owned premises could be licensed for marriage ceremonies. This would lead to an increasing trend for couples to marry away from their place of birth.

1996
OPCS becomes part of the new ONS.

1999
Separate parliaments begin in Wales, Scotland and Northern Ireland.

House of Lords Act - inherited peerages stop.

2000s

2000
Freedom of Information Act - people can now access records; even ones closed under 30 year rule.

2001
Sunday 29 April. National Census. Approximately 94% of the population was recorded.

2002
Nationality, Immigration and Asylum Act permitted children born overseas to British mothers registration as UK citizens.

The Land Registration Act brought further change to existing procedures of recording land conveyance. Details of land ownership can be accessed from Her Majesty's Land Registry.

Freedom of Information (Scotland) Act.

2003
TNA was created, by combining the PRO with the HMC and OPSI.

2004
Enlargement of the EU led to many thousands of Poles and others from Eastern Europe to come to Britain.

2005
From 30 December it is now legal to trace adopted people via an Intermediary Agency.

Same-sex civil partnerships begin.

2011
Sunday 27 March. National census.

2000
Worst flooding in Britain since records began in 1850

2001
11 September – World Trade Centre attack – 9/11

Population 59 million

2003
(to 2010) Gulf War Two

2004
Only 13 coal mines left open (169 in 1984)

2005
London suicide bombers - 7/7

IRA declare an end to their armed struggle

2007
(to 2010) Gordon Brown, Labour

2010
(to present) David Cameron, Conservative, Nick Clegg Liberal Democrat (Coalition)

2011
Riots across Britain

Population 62.4 million

News of the World closes

SELECT INDEX

The subjects listed below cover most of the entries in the timeline. Search for the subject you require and you will see the relevant date or dates under which information may be found.

Deeds Registries – 1704
Directories – 1734, 1763, 1772, 1773, 1791, 1814, 1817, 1820, 1826, 1831,
   1833, 1845, 1846 (medical), 1858 (Crockford's), 1880 (telephone)
Disease: 1846, 1895, 1952
  cholera – 1816, 1831, 1832, 1848, 1853, 1866
  diphtheria – 1858, 1859
  influenza – 1918
  plague – 1349, 1563, 1603-4, 1665
  smallpox – 1838, 1853, 1855, 1871
  sweating sickness – 1485, 1517, 1528, 1551
  typhus – 1847
Divorce – 1536, 1670, 1830, 1857, 1923, 1937, 1969
Doomsday Survey – 1086
Drake, Sir Francis – 1577
East Africa – 1920s
East India Company – 1600
Ecclesiastical lists – 1711, 1858
Education and schools: 1811, 1823, 1870, 1880, 1988
 schools – 1547, 1552, 1698, 1811, 1816, 1818 (Ragged), 1870, 1876,
   1880, 1893, 1900, 1902, 1918, 1944, 1947
 universities – 1167, 1209, 1230,1823, 1826 (London), 1870, 1920
Electoral registers – 1832, 1835, 1884
Emigration – 1609, 1630, 1682, 1792, 1796, 1803, 1816, 1828, 1830's, 1845,
   1847, 1862, 1945, 1957, 1969
Enclosure of land – 1489, 1516, 1549, 1761
Factories – 1771, 1833, 1844, 1874
Famine – 1315, 1369, 1586, 1709, 1730, 1740, 1795, 1845
Farming – 1794, 1827, 1870
Feet of Fines – 1187
Fine Rolls – 1272
Freemen Rolls – c1266
Fire insurance records – 1710
Foundling Hospital – 1741
Franchise – 1832, 1867, 1869, 1884, 1918, 1928
Friendly societies – 1793
General Register Office – 1836
Glebe terrier – 1571
Gold rush – 1848, 1851
Gravestones – later 1600s
Gregorian calendar – 1581, 1600, 1752
Guilds – 1100s, 1388
Gunpowder – 1242
Gypsies – 1530, 1551, 1554, 1662
Heraldry – 1127, 1483/4, 1530, 1798
Highland clearances – 1752, 1792, 1811
Hong Kong – 1842

Masonic lodge – 171
Mayorial records – 1290
Medical registers – 1859
Memorial brasses – 1200s
Militia – 1285, 1757, 1793, 1795, 1796, 1798, 1799, 1803, 1812, 1814
Mining – 1842
Monasteries – 1070, 1128, 1130, 1143, 1177, 1221, 1224, 1536
Mormonism – 1830
Muster Rolls – 1522, 1630, 1708, 1732
Navy and merchant seamen – 1525, 1590, 1660, 1667, 1668, 1673, 1691,
                                   1695, 1772, 1782, 1795, 1803, 1814, 1835,
                                   1853, 1869, 1884
Newspapers & periodicals – 1622, 1665, 1702, 1718, 1731, 1739, 1772, 1785,
                                   1842, 1849, 1855
New towns – 1277
New Zealand – 1769, 1820
Non-conformity: 1650, 1664, 1672, 1676, 1689, 1695, 1742, 1898
         Congregationalists (Brownists) – 1580, 1644
         Lutheran – 1669
         Methodism – 1739, 1780
         Moravian – 1741
         Plymouth Brethren – 1830
         Presbyterianism – 1570's
         Quakerism – 1648, 1662
         Unitarianism – 1762
         United Reform Church – 1972
Oath of Allegiance – 1641
Old Bailey – 1674
Parish records (baptismal, marriage and funeral) & registers – 1538, 1550,
                                   1558, 1598, 1634, 1695, 1698, 1812, 1831
Patent Rolls – 1202
Pipe Rolls – 1130
Pilgrim Fathers – 1620
Photography – 1835, 1860, 1865
Plague *(see Disease)*
Poll Books – 1696, 1832, 1835, 1872
Poor – 1388, 1494, 1531, 1536, 1547, 1552, 1562, 1563, 1576, 1597, 1601,
         1647, 1662, 1687, 1762, 1766, 1795 (Speenhamland), 1818, 1834,
         1838, 1840, 1845, 1884, 1889, 1948
Prison – 1628, 1676, 1770, 1779, 1824, 1869
Probate – 1857, 1858, 1898, 1949
Protestation Oath – 1641
Public Record Office – 1838
Puritans – 1630
Quarter Session Records – 1388, 1581
Railways – 1804, 1825, 1830, 1837, 1840, 1844, 1863 (London Underground)

Rate books – 1601, 1868
Rebellions, revolts and riots: 1525, 1538, 1780, 1792, 1795, 1839, 1981, 1985,
1990, 2011
       Chartist – 1838
       Glorious – 1688
       Jacobite – 1719, 1745
       Indian – 1857
       Irish – 1641
       Kett's – 1549,
       Luddite – 1811, 1814
       Midland – 1607,
       Northern – 1569,
       Peasants' Revolt – 1381
       Peterloo – 1819
       Pilgrimage of Grace – 1536
       Rebecca – 1839
       Swing – 1830
       Ulster – 1642
       Western – 1547
       Wyatt's – 1553
Recusants – 1581, 1592, 1676
Reformation – 1534
Refugees *(see Immigrants)*
Register of Sasines – 1617
Salvation Army – 1865, 1885
Schools *(see Education)*
Scotland – 1296, 1536, 1560, 1574, 1611, 1617, 1672, 1741, 1752, 1824,
             1845, 1846, 1854, 1855, 1865, 1867, 1868, 1876, 1882, 1929,
             1969, 1973, 1994, 1999
Settlement certificates – 1601, 1662, 1697
Simon de Montfort – 1265
Singapore – 1819
Slavery – 1441, 1788, 1807, 1812, 1833
South Africa – 1660, 1867
Spa towns – 1626
Suffragettes – 1903, 1911, 1913
Surnames – 1130, 1400s
Tasmania – 1803, 1856
Taxation – 1288, 1290, 1341, 1377, 1379, 1381, 1523, 1525, 1549, 1597,
          1634, 1642, 1660, 1661, 1662 (Hearth), 1693, 1696 (Window),
          1710, 1747, 1777, 1783, 1784, 1785, 1795, 1796 (Death duty),
          1798 (Income), 1851, 1906 (Inheritance), 1975, 1990, 1991
Temperance societies – 1820s
Thomas Becket – 1170
Tithe Applotment Books – 1823
Tithes – 1836